THE WATERFALLS OF ENGLAND

A practical guide for visitors and walkers

Griff J. Fellows

Line drawings by Lynne Dunnett

From the waterfall he named her,
Minnehaha, Laughing Water.

– The Song of Hiawatha
Henry Wadsworth Longfellow (1855)

Published by Sigma Leisure – an imprint of
Sigma Press, 5 Alton Road, Wilmslow, Cheshire SK9 5DY, England.

British Library Cataloguing in Publication Data
A CIP record for this book is available from the British Library.

ISBN: 1-85058-767-1

Typesetting and Design by: Sigma Press, Wilmslow, Cheshire.

Printed by: Interprint Ltd, Malta

Cover Photograph: Hardraw Force; note the author near the base of the fall

Cover Design: Sigma Leisure, Wilmslow

Photographs: the author, except where indicated

Maps: Section maps by PerroCarto. Individual waterfall location maps by the author – reproduced from Ordnance Survey mapping on behalf of The Controller of Her Majesty's Stationery Office © Crown Copyright Licence Number MC 100032058.

Illustrations: Lynne Dunnett

DISCLAIMER

Foreword

– by Mike Harding

In Praise of Waterfalls

The ancient Celts revered waterfalls as very special places where spirits could cross over from the other world. Jennet's Foss near Gordale Scar in the Yorkshire Dales is one such fall, named (so it is said) after an undine or water sprite called Jenny. Perhaps she was the same Jenny that we were taunted with as children – only our Jenny was called Jinny Greenteeth and she lived down the drainage grids in the busy Manchester streets.

In Nepal I have walked in the high Himalaya and come across waterfalls with shrines before them and when I asked the sherpas why the shrines were there I was told that a very powerful spirit lived in that place and the shrines were there for the worship of the spirit.

And even now in our modern high-tech society with its internet cafés and interactive TV, its fast cars and its great city lights that banish all spirits and daemons to the shadows, we are still fascinated by waterfalls. High falls, wide falls, massive torrents and gentle streams – the sound of running water falling draws us still.

In this book you will find everything you need to know about waterfalls: how they are formed, what lives under them; what good they do and how to find them and walk to them amongst other things.

So take this book, some sandwiches and somebody special (preferably an unabashed child or two) and go and sit on a summer's day by one of the great falls. Say nothing and listen to what it has to say to you.

Mike Harding

Entertainer, travel writer and photographer (amongst other things), Mike Harding was born in Manchester and is widely respected for his support of ecological and environmental issues. A fellow of the Royal Geographical Society, Mike was President of The Ramblers Association for three years and is now a lifetime Vice President.

Preface

Waterfalls have universal appeal. They are dramatic features along the course of rivers and streams and are usually set in beautiful scenery. They hold special interest for walkers, artists, geologists and naturalists. The preliminary chapters introduce the reader to the geology, flora and fauna, power generation and other uses, art and poetry of waterfalls.

The body of the book lists and describes nearly 200 of the best waterfalls in England starting in the far north in Northumberland and working south all the way to Cornwall. Only falls that are natural and with public access have been included.

Each fall is described according to a standard pattern. The name of the fall is followed by a star rating ☆ to ☆☆☆☆☆. This is unavoidably subjective and, no doubt will give rise to disagreement!

☆☆☆☆☆ – a spectacular waterfall, one of the best of its type, in a beautiful setting.

☆☆☆☆ – a dramatic fall with exceptional features.

☆☆☆ – an attractive fall with no displeasing features.

☆☆ – a pleasant fall, likely to be small.

☆ – a small fall, included because it is in an area where there are few waterfalls or it has exceptionally easy access.

An Ordnance Survey (OS) grid reference, a small map and distances from the nearest towns locate the fall accurately. A compass bearing is a guide to photographers to suggest the best time of day to view the falls. Wheelchair access is indicated. The walk to the falls is graded according to severity:

Easy – no steep gradients and a relatively smooth walking surface, no special footwear required.

Moderate – muddy or stony paths and/or short steep gradients. Stout shoes or walking boots needed.

Difficult – long steep gradients, scrambles or indistinct paths.

However, a moderately fit person will be able to reach all these falls. The approximate time to walk to the fall and back is given.

Each fall is briefly described and illustrated. Line drawings highlight items of interest. Instructions are given to reach each fall from a suitable parking place. This is not primarily a walking guide and readers are encouraged to incorporate the falls into walks which they have planned themselves, preferably using public transport whenever feasible. Features of local interest are mentioned.

A word about left and right. The left bank of a river is the one to your left when facing downstream. This applies above, through and below a waterfall. Therefore, when looking upstream at a waterfall, the left bank of the waterfall is to your right, just like looking at someone's face – easy!

I have thoroughly enjoyed visiting these waterfalls in all seasons of the year and my wish is that you have similar pleasure from these dramatic natural features set in some of England's most stunning scenery.

Acknowledgements

The painting by J. M. W. Turner of Hardraw Fall is reproduced with permission of the Fitzwilliam Museum, University of Cambridge and the painting entitled *Waterfall* by Arshile Gorky with permission of the Tate Modern Art Gallery and the Design and Artists Copyright Society.

I am grateful to authors and publishers for permission to include extracts of several poems. The excerpt from the poem by Norman Nicholson entitled *Beck* is from his book, *Selected Poems 1940–1982* published by Faber and Faber. The lines from *Behind the Waterfall* by Hilary Llewellyn-Williams are from *Animaculture* published by Seren Books in 1997. The whole poem *Gray Wagtail* is reproduced from *Collected Poems* by Norman MacCaig published by Chatto and Windus, used by permission of The Random House Group Limited. I am indebted to Elizabeth Corner for reading the chapter on poetry and for her helpful suggestions.

I would also thank Dr Christine Whittingham of the Open University for reading the chapter on geology and for her constructive criticisms.

Barbara Thompson and other staff of the Witt Library, The Courtauld Institute of Fine Art allowed me access to their extensive records and were most helpful in tracking down artists and paintings and deserve my thanks.

I would like to thank Anthony Gresford for advice from his store of knowledge of the world of publishing.

I thank all those who have pointed me in the direction of waterfalls that I might otherwise have missed. These include Hazel Holland, Ted Liddle and John Firby, but also many others with whom I had fleeting conversations and whose names I never recorded.

A thank you to my brother, Thomas Fellows, for the photograph of the 'La'al Ratty' engine in waterfall number 68. My daughter, Lynne Dunnett, deserves a huge thank you for her line drawings which she managed to do aided and abetted by her young family. These drawings add life to the pages and enhance the whole book. My wife, Scilla, has given invaluable suggestions throughout the gestation period of this book. Many were the times we walked together on fells and hills in all weathers — thank you for your company on those occasions and for your constant encouragement.

Griff Fellows

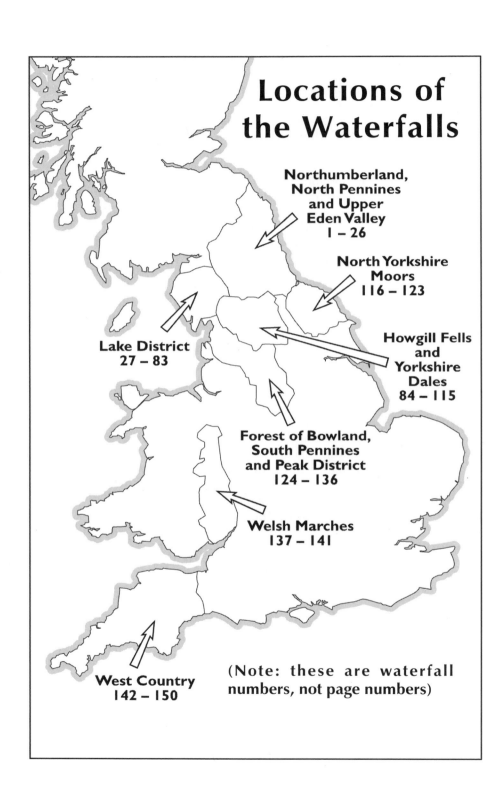

Locations of the Waterfalls

Northumberland, North Pennines and Upper Eden Valley 1 – 26

North Yorkshire Moors 116 – 123

Howgill Fells and Yorkshire Dales 84 – 115

Lake District 27 – 83

Forest of Bowland, South Pennines and Peak District 124 – 136

Welsh Marches 137 – 141

West Country 142 – 150

(Note: these are waterfall numbers, not page numbers)

Contents

1.

Dangers and Delights

Dangers

This bit is important! Waterfalls are dangerous places and due care must be taken. They are often in steep-sided ravines. Wet rocks can be incredibly slippery, more so than rocks at the seaside. Plunge pools are often very deep, sometimes as deep as the falls are high. Beneath a large waterfall the water sweeps back in a vertical rotary motion pulling a swimmer on the surface towards the fall. It is tempting to go under a waterfall to cool off on a hot summer's day. Remember that streams are continuously eroding their beds and moving material downstream. Think what a pebble would do to your head!

Weather changes rapidly. On a hot sunny morning, go prepared for a cold rainy afternoon. Take a good map and compass. Tell someone else where you are going and by what route. Do not rely on a mobile phone to call for help – there may be no signal. For both safety and the enjoyment of others, obey the Countryside Code:

Enjoy the countryside and respect the life and work of those who live there.
Guard against risk of fire.
Fasten all gates.
Keep dogs under close control.
Keep to public paths across farmland.
Do not damage fences, hedges and walls; always and only use gates and stiles.
Leave no litter.
Do not contaminate any water supplies.
Protect wildlife, plants and trees.
Take special care on country roads.
Make no unnecessary noise.

Delights

It is a rare person who sees no beauty in a waterfall. A waterfall is the most dramatic natural event along the course of a river or stream. A lazy, placid and silent stream suddenly drops vertically over a cliff causing a chaos of spray and noise, then quickly reverts to its previous character a few yards downstream.

Waterfalls are as varied as anything in nature. Some impress, or even overwhelm, by their sheer power, particularly when in spate. Although in England we have no falls as wide as Niagara or carrying the same volume of water (we do have falls that are considerably higher), we still have falls whose power makes the heart beat faster.

Some falls enchant by their grace and beauty, a diaphanous veil of white against a background of dark rock, or a number of streams separating and rejoining forming a pattern as intricate as lace. Some form simple columns of unbroken water. Some show perfect symmetry falling from ledge to ledge each wider than the one above, like a multi-tiered wedding cake. Others, no less beautiful, have a totally random, irregular shape as the water is thrown from one slab of rock to another as it falls.

Often set within ravines that they have carved out of the bedrock over thousands of years, waterfalls provide havens of peace and tranquillity. A small fall in a hollow, sheltered from wind, providing a microclimate for mosses, ferns and flowering plants is an oasis on a bleak mountainside.

England's landscape is built on a human scale. There is no part that cannot be reached within a day and still have time to get back to civilisation for dinner. We may not have a Victoria Falls, but we can still share something of what David Livingstone felt when he was the first European to see the falls that he named after his queen and which the local Kololo people call *Mosi-oa-Tunya*, 'The Smoke that Thunders'. He wrote, 'The most wonderful sight I had seen in Africa ... scenes so lovely must have been gazed upon by angels in their flight.'

2.

How waterfalls form

Waterfalls are not constant features in the landscape. In the geological time-scale they are short-lived affairs. They are always on the move travelling towards the source of the stream. Waterfalls only require three conditions: running water, relatively hard rock and a cliff.

Running water

One advantage of the English climate is that rain falls all the year round and most streams and rivers do not run dry. Spates can happen at any time. Nearly all the world's water is held in the oceans and polar ice-caps. The remainder is in underground aquifers, surface water (lakes, rivers, ice-fields and glaciers), in the biosphere and in the atmosphere. When rain falls some water is absorbed into the ground and some remains on the surface to form streams, the proportion will depend on the nature of the soil and underlying rock. Vegetation acts as a sponge to hold water and release it slowly. The hill walker will find boggy ground even when hose-pipe bans are in force.

Human activity can profoundly affect the flow of streams and rivers. Damming a stream to form a reservoir has a similar effect to vegetation; the flow is evened out, spates reduced, but the stream is less likely to run dry. However, excessive water extraction may cause a stream to dry up.

Relatively hard rock

Clearly the lip of a waterfall must be made of hard rock, otherwise it would erode very quickly. What rocks in England are hard enough and where did they come from? They have all been formed over the last 600 million years during which the portion of the Earth's crust that would eventually become England has been subjected to the force of colliding tectonic plates, experienced prolonged and violent volcanic eruptions, baked under arid desert conditions, sunk beneath the sea several times and – quite recently on the geological time-scale – has been scoured by great glaciers. The account of these processes is fascinating, but outside the scope of this book.

The landscape of England has been eroded by ice intermittently for the last two million years. We are now living in an interglacial period. As will be described, waterfalls are abundant in landscapes subjected to glaciation.

Rocks that are hard enough to form the tops of waterfalls are numerous. They include sedimentary rocks (sandstones, limestones), igneous rocks (tuffs, lavas, granite, dolorite) and metamorphic rocks (slates) to mention just a few. The identification of rocks in the field is rewarding, but often difficult.

Handbooks illustrating different rocks and regional field-guides, of which there are many, are invaluable.

The rock determines the appearance of the landscape and also the type of waterfall that is likely to be found. Almost horizontal beds of limestone alternating with softer shales form the characteristic landscape of the Yorkshire Dales termed 'karst'. The sides of the flat-topped hills are stepped and often the limestone forms inland cliffs called 'scars'. Flat limestone surfaces devoid of soil cover are termed pavements. Cracks ('grikes') in the pavements give shelter to rare lime-loving plants. Rainwater is a very dilute solution of carbonic acid formed from dissolved carbon dioxide derived from the atmosphere. This water gradually dissolves limestone and over millennia will produce underground channels and caverns. Sometimes a stream drops into a hole (pot) in the ground such as at Gaping Gill. Even rivers running along valley floors may sink into the ground to emerge on the surface further downstream. The River Dee in Dentdale is an example. Rivers in limestone dales are often wide and shallow producing correspondingly wide waterfalls as they tumble over limestone ledges (e.g. Wain Wath Falls and Aysgarth Falls). Streams dropping over high limestone scars form semicircular amphitheatres as at Hardraw and the hard lip of the fall may project and throw the stream clear of the rock face. The darker millstone grit and sandstones of the Southern Pennines give the landscape a more sombre appearance.

The northern part of the Lake District and the southern, together with the Howgill Fells, are composed of sedimentary rocks laid down on ocean floors. The contours of these hills are rounded. In contrast, the central area of the Lake District is formed from volcanoes that erupted with considerable violence, similar to Mount St Helens in 1982. This has produced a landscape of great complexity and ruggedness.

The Cheviot volcano erupted in a more gentle fashion and has largely been overlain with sedimentary rocks, giving a much smoother landscape to that part of Northumberland.

In density terms, granite is a relatively light rock and tends to rise through the upper part of the Earth's crust lifting the rocks above it. Several upland areas of England are raised on huge masses of granite termed 'batholiths.' When overlying rocks have eroded away then the granite is exposed. This process has occurred in the Cheviot Hills, Lake District and South-west Peninsular. Another example of igneous intrusion is worthy of mention, the Great Whin Sill. Molten rock rose up and was then forced horizontally between beds of sedimentary rock beneath a large area of the north of England. This Whin Stone (Dolerite) is extremely hard and resistant to erosion. It forms the rock of many waterfalls including High Force in Teesdale.

Glaciation (except in the south of England) produced the landscape we see today. Valleys were deepened, straightened and converted to a U-shaped cross-section by moving glaciers. Large quantities of boulder clay were deposited in low-lying regions.

Cliffs

When a stream runs over a bed of hard rock why should it suddenly find itself plummeting over a cliff? In practice, virtually all waterfall cliffs are formed by erosion. Previously land continued beyond the present waterfall and some geological process has removed or displaced it. We will briefly consider four processes.

Erosion by the stream itself

The present form of a waterfall is the result of the stream eroding its bed. Throughout the length of a stream, there is a balance between erosion in fast flow conditions and deposition when the flow is sluggish. Waterfalls migrate upstream (getting smaller as they go) because of the erosive action of water both at the lip and the base of the falls. The net result is that a smooth profile tends to form from source to mouth. If there is a sudden fall in sea (or lake) level the profile at the mouth will steepen, resulting in a waterfall or rapids. This then migrates upstream at what is termed a 'knick point' (see Figure 2.1).

A waterfall will form when a stream flows over hard rock onto softer rock which is more easily eroded. What processes can bring harder and softer rocks into proximity along the bed of a stream? One is the deposition of veins of hard crystalline rock within a softer rock. Figure 2.2 shows this on a small scale as a stream crosses a vein of quartz within slate. The same effect is produced by igneous intrusions, sometimes on a huge scale, such as the Great Whin Sill at High Force on the River Tees and several other northern waterfalls.

Another way in which a stream can flow across rocks of different hardness, thus producing the conditions for a waterfall to form, is by the process of fault-

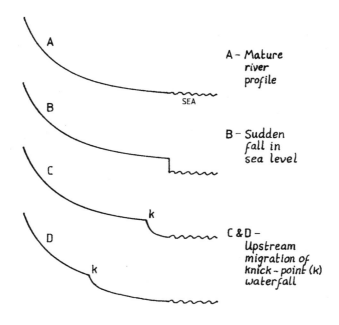

Figure 2.1 Regression of a waterfall at its knick-point.

Figure 2.2 Small waterfall over a vein of quartz in Rocky Valley, Cornwall.

ing. A build-up of pressure within the earth's crust leads to fracture and movement of one part relative to another. This can bring softer rock into horizontal contact with harder rock. Figure 2.3 shows how this happens. 'A' represents the situation before faulting begins. A stream flows on relatively soft rock from left to right. In 'B' and 'C' faulting starts and continues very slowly. The stream has plenty of time to smooth out surface irregularities and erode through the soft rock of its bed. Finally in 'D' it has worn down to the hard rock upstream, but erosion of the soft rock downstream continues and a waterfall is formed. Folly Dolly Falls near Huddersfield shows this process clearly.

Erosion by a larger river or glacier

A large river or glacier has greater erosive force and, therefore, carves a deeper valley than smaller tributary streams whose valleys are left high above the main valley. These 'hanging valleys' are drained by streams which form waterfalls as they drop to the main valley floor, often cutting back ravines into the hillsides. If the side walls of the large valley are composed of alternating beds of, say, limestone and shale, then a tributary stream from a hanging

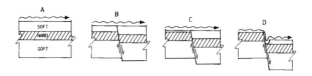

Figure 2.3 Waterfall caused by faulting.

valley will erode the shale faster than the limestone and form a series of water-falls down the hillside.

Hanging valleys and their associated waterfalls are commonly found in glaciated landscapes such as the Lake District. Occasionally, though, the erosion of the main valley is due entirely to the action of water; Lydford Gorge in Devon is one example.

Erosion by the sea

Along the north-west Devon coast the sea has eroded the land so fast that the lower courses of streams have been washed away. The result is a series of waterfalls over coastal cliffs. Occasionally the sea has cut into the side of a valley, capturing the stream, the remaining course of the valley being dry.

Erosion by human activity

Several waterfalls in England have been formed by quarrying. Segments of hillside are removed leaving vertical cliffs across the beds of streams. Examples are seen near Coniston on Torver Beck and in Weardale on a tributary of Stanhope Burn.

Waterfalls do not just happen. It is a fascinating exercise to try and work out from the signs in the rocks and the landscape the reasons why they are there.

3.

Waterfalls put to use

Agriculture

If it's there, someone will find a use for it and, if possible, make a profit out of it. The first to do so with waterfalls were farmers. Plunge pools beneath water-falls have been used to wash stock. Sheep used to be washed at Janet's Foss near Malham. The whole community took part; the farmers working waist deep in icy water while their women folk supplied them with copious quanti-ties of ale to keep out the cold.

Water extraction and storage

The pool below a waterfall is a convenient site to place a pipe to extract water and take it by gravity down to the settle-ment in the valley. If water is to be extracted on a larger scale then a dam and reservoir must be built. Waterfalls may occur where a ridge of hard rock crosses a valley. The valley may be

Figure 3.1 Small scale water extraction

narrow at this site where the stream or river has eroded the hard rock more slowly than softer rock up and down stream. This would then be a suitable place to dam the river and create a reservoir. An example is Cauldron Snout where the River Tees crosses part of the Great Whin Sill. Just above Cauldron Snout a dam, which is partly built on the Great Whin Sill, holds back the water in Cow Green Reservoir.

Power

The force of flowing or falling water has been harnessed since, at least, Roman times. The Greek Mill was the first known design. Water was channelled to one side of a wheel mounted horizontally. From this, a shaft passed vertically up through the centre of a fixed stone to an upper stone that rotated. Grinding of corn was the earliest use of water power. The Norse Mill using the same design as the Greek mill was operational in parts of Britain as late as the 19th century. Vitruvius, writing between 20 and 13 BC, described in detail an undershot waterwheel mounted vertically. These waterwheels utilise the kinetic energy of moving water and achieved efficiencies of around 30%. Overshot wheels were more efficient (80%) but needed a greater height of water. This was readily available at waterfalls. With a greater head of water the wheel diameter could be increased and more power generated. Overshot and pitchback wheels harnessed the potential energy of the water and carried buckets rather than paddles. An advantage of pitchback wheels was that the water in the tail-race flowed in the direction of rotation of the wheel. A pitchback wheel can be seen at Rutter Force, number 26. Many refinements were made to increase their efficiency. General J. V. Poncelet produced curved paddles for undershot wheels and lowered the tail-race to avoid back-watering.

By the end of the 18th century, there were waterwheels capable of an

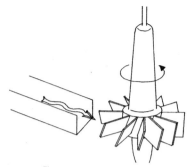

Figure 3.2 Norse Wheel

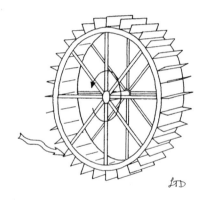

Figure 3.3 Undershot Wheel

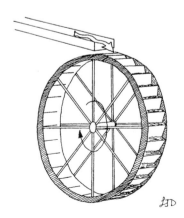

Figure 3.4 Overshot Wheel

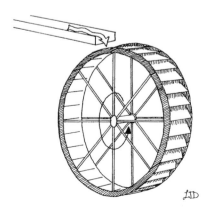

Figure 3.5 Pitchback Wheel

excess of 100 horsepower. The 19th century saw the development of water turbines that did not require the large water flows of the older waterwheels, which then fell into disuse. Water power, however, continued for many years after the steam engine was invented.

Many watermills were productive for centuries, although their products changed. One at Troutbeck Bridge near Windermere was a fulling-mill till 1390, a corn-mill, a paper-mill, a flax-mill, a bobbin-mill and finally generated electricity until 1947. Other uses of water power included crushing and smelting ores, pumping water out of mines, manufacture of gunpowder, paper making and drawing wire.

Although many of the wheels have gone, the remains of buildings and leats can often be found in the vicinity of waterfalls.

Sport

Climbing frozen waterfalls is a popular sport when winters are cold enough. We will have to wait and see whether climate change will put a stop to that sport in England. Twenty people have deliberately gone over Niagara Falls in a variety of containers and fifteen survived to describe the experience. Fortunately, this sport has not taken on in Britain!

Tourism

Hard on the heels of the industrial revolution followed a number of factors which led to the development of the tourist industry. People living in towns had money and leisure, although little by today's standards. Railways opened up the countryside to day-trippers. Romantic authors and poets such as Walter Scott and William Wordsworth enabled people to view nature in new ways and drew them into the countryside. There was an increase in interest in natural history, arts and crafts and folklore. Rambling and cycling societies were established. By the late 19th century, footpath preservation groups were commonplace. Large tracts of privately owned upland countryside remained closed to the public. Several mass trespasses, like the one of 1932 onto Kinder Scout in Derbyshire, persuaded land owners to open up their moorlands for public recreation. Waterfalls were popular destinations for tourists in Victorian times, particularly those that had featured in paintings and poetry and had easy access by road or rail. Lodore falls and Aira Force in the Lake District and Hardraw Force and Aysgarth Falls in the Yorkshire Dales were among the most frequented, and still are. Approximately twice as many tourists spend nights in the countryside as in small and large towns put together. Nature, waterfalls included, shows no sign of losing its appeal.

One other use

I have seen one waterfall (not in England) which was previously used as a gallows. Those convicted of murder and the like were simply pushed over the top.

4.

Plants and Wildlife around Waterfalls

All living things are part of food chains. Bacteria and fungi on a decaying leaf trapped beneath a stone release nutrients for algae on the surface of the stone. Invertebrate larvae feed off the algae and are, in turn, food for trout caught by a fisherman. Algae play a crucial part in the ecology of fast-flowing streams and without them these streams would support very little life at all.

A section of stream is not a closed ecological system. Living organisms move up and down stream, organic matter is swept down by the current and there is interchange of material, not only with life on the banks of the stream, but further afield.

Influence of waterfalls

Waterfalls influence the environment, and hence plant and animal life, in a number of ways. First, they form barriers to the movement of aquatic life both up and down stream. Trout and, particularly, salmon are able to leap smaller waterfalls. Eels slither up wet rock surfaces and vegetation beside falls. All these species survive the downward journey. Surprisingly, most microcrustacea and other plankton do not survive being swept over large falls. Secondly falling water entraps air bubbles and increases the concentration of dissolved oxygen and carbon dioxide. Oxygen is essential for all animal life and carbon dioxide is absorbed and utilised by plants. Mosses and liverworts need a high concentration of dissolved carbon dioxide. Thirdly waterfalls convert dissolved organic matter by flocculation to fine particulate organic matter making it available to invertebrate species that filter out their diet from the water flow, certain species of caddis fly larvae for example. Fourthly, waterfalls often erode gullies or ravines which provides shelter from wind and enables trees, and other plants, to flourish which could not survive on the adjacent hillside. Fifthly, waterfalls produce spray - providing a constant damp environment suitable for ferns, mosses, liverworts and other plants. Lastly, waterfalls are dangerous places. Many species have adapted to this harsh environment and thus have escaped from their predators. Some of these adaptations are discussed later.

It is beyond the scope of this short chapter to describe any species in detail or their inter-relationships. The reader is encouraged to observe in the field and to read any of the excellent books on plant and animal life that have been published. Only the commoner types and species will be mentioned. The habitat beside waterfalls harbours rare plants of interest to botanists.

Non-flowering plants

Rocks around waterfalls, including the lip of the falls, are slippery due to a film of algae. Many species are found, both felt forming and filamentous varieties. This biofilm also contains bacteria harmless to humans. It is the primary food source for several species of insect larvae, snails and freshwater limpets. This is the principal pathway linking vegetable and animal life in this environment.

The splash zones of waterfalls provide suitable conditions for liverworts and mosses. Liverworts are found towards the headwaters of streams. The number of species of moss increases further downstream. Different species have different habitats. Some are truly aquatic, some intermittently inundated and others are terrestrial. Mosses provide shelter and refuge from strong currents for a great variety of invertebrate life, rotifers, protozoa and insect larvae for example, and food for some, such as water bears (Tardigrades). Lichens are algae and fungi living in a symbiotic relationship. Map lichens form characteristic patches, often yellow or grey/white on boulders. Beard lichens festoon branches of trees in damp environments such as ravines and are sensitive indicators of atmospheric pollution.

Moist sheltered conditions around waterfalls in ravines are ideal for ferns that can tolerate shade. Their forms and sizes vary greatly. The Tunbridge Filmy Fern, with translucent fronds of just a few centimetres length found embedded in moss cushions in the splash zone of waterfalls, contrasts sharply with the majestic Royal Fern whose fronds can stretch more than two metres. Some, such as Broad Buckler Fern are evergreen, others like Male Fern with its characteristic 'crosiers' in the spring die down completely for the winter. Oak fern, mountain fern, lady fern and the dainty parsley fern (the latter found in drier habitats on screes and walls) all prefer acid conditions. Hard shield fern and spleenwort thrive in base-rich environments, as does the maidenhair fern on alkaline sea cliffs.

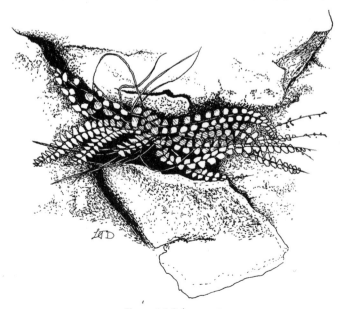

Figure 4.1 Spleenwort

Flowering plants

Flowering plants common to the adjacent moorland, woodland or coastal cliffs form natural rock gardens alongside waterfalls.

Damp conditions attract other species. Water avens with graceful, reddish pendulous flowers are found along streams. In Yorkshire and Durham look out for the rose-pink flower heads of bird's-eye primrose. The flower of the carnivorous common butterwort, borne on a single stalk, is seen springing from a star shaped rosette of pale green leaves on damp soil beside streams. Several members of the dead-nettle family may be found, particularly the hand-some marsh woundwort. Drifts of monkey flower (Mimulus) give a splash of bright yellow. The plants were introduced to Britain from Alaska in the 18th century, but thrive along the banks of northern streams and rivers. Other conspicuous colourful foreign introductions to streamsides are orange balsam, also from North Amer-ica, and the larger, brasher, Indian (Himalayan) balsam.

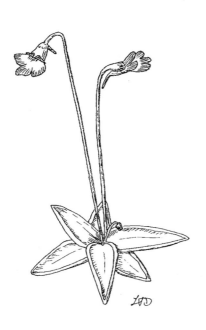

Figure 4.2 Common Butterwort

Britain sports only three native conifers (admittedly, they are not flowering plants): Scots pine, common juniper and yew. Juniper bushes frequently over-hang waterfalls at higher altitudes than other trees. The berry-like cones take two to three years to ripen. The stems are often twisted into fantastic shapes. Rowan (mountain ash) is the tree most frequently seen scattered along the gullies carved by waterfalls down steep hillsides, particularly on acid soils. The pinnate leaves, more delicate than those of ash, large white flower heads and bunches of bright red berries make it a most attractive tree. Common ash has a similar distribution, particularly in limestone country. Hawthorn is equally hardy and found high on mountain-sides. Other common trees along upland streams are silver birch, alder and holly. Further downstream in wooded valleys oak, beech and the non-native sycamore come into their own.

Invertebrates

The principal herbivorous fauna in the environment of waterfalls are small invertebrates living on the bed of the stream (the 'benthic' environment). These include insect larvae, crustaceans and molluscs. The larvae of stoneflies (Plecoptera) tolerate low temperature, low oxygen and low nutrient concen-trations. They are, therefore, found further upstream that most other orders. They have two 'tails' (see figure 4.3). Mayfly larvae (Ephemeroptera) have three 'tails'. The larvae of numerous species of caddis fly (Trichoptera) form

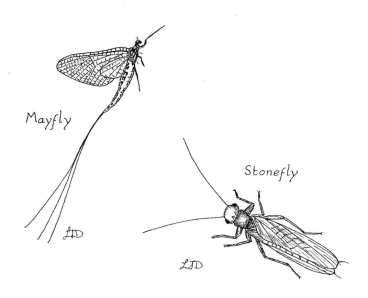

Figure 4.3 Mayfly and Stonefly

cases from small pebbles or debris, which protect them from predators. True flies (Diptera) include midges. Their larvae have a wide distribution. Many attach themselves to stones by means of suckers. Others show different adaptations to life in fast flowing water. Some attach themselves to 'silk' mats, which they weave on stones. Others have flattened, streamlined bodies. (Yet shrimps, for instance, are neither streamlined nor flattened, but cope perfectly well with fast flow!) Some larvae are equipped with tiny hooks to cling onto the substrate. Molluscs comprise snails, freshwater limpets and mussels. Not all these invertebrates are herbivores. According to their feeding methods they can be described as scrapers (snails and many insect larvae living off films of algae); shredders (coarse particulate organic matter e.g. leaf fragments); collectors (fine particulate organic matter and debris wafted to their mouthparts or caught in 'silk' nets); piercers (which live off mosses and other aquatic plants); predators and parasites.

Why are not all small organisms washed downstream and end up in the sea? In addition to the methods of attachment already described, it should be mentioned that many organisms are capable of upstream movement. Also the adult, breeding stage of many insects fly upstream to deposit their eggs. Many larvae are washed downstream (drift), especially at night and during spates when they fall prey to trout and other fish. Drift is not an entirely passive process as larvae can, to some extent, control drift distances. It is a mechanism that assures even distribution of the species.

Vertebrates

Many upland waterfalls are higher than any fish can reach. Of the 42 native

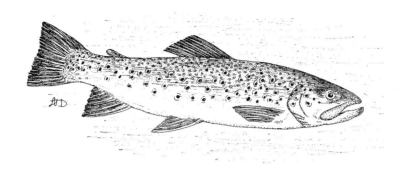

Figure 4.4 Brown Trout

freshwater species in Britain those that penetrate furthest upstream are trout, salmon, bullhead (miller's thumb), minnow and stone loach. These inhabit the 'trout zone' where water flow is fast and the stream bed made of rock and shingle. Brown trout, which live out their whole life cycle in fresh water, can interbreed with sea trout that return to streams to spawn. In summer the main food of trout is insects and caterpillars that have dropped onto the surface of the water. In winter, they survive on shrimps and other benthic invertebrates. One of the finest sights to see at a waterfall is salmon leaping to spawn upstream. This is always by day as they aim at the top of the fall by sight. To assist them, they leap from the crest of the standing wave at the base of the fall, using the up-current on the downstream portion of the wave. A salmon hen may lay 5 000 eggs in one redd, the hollow she forms in the gravel. Most will hatch, but only 1 per cent will reach the sea.

Birds to see around waterfalls are those from the surrounding habitat, moorland, mountain crags, woodland or sea-shore. Some species, though, confine themselves largely to the course of the stream. The grey wagtail is a bird of fast flowing streams, (whereas the yellow wagtail prefers marshland). This energetic bird is never still. The male wears a black bib in the summer when the yellow on the rump and under the tail extends further onto the belly. It feeds off invertebrates in shallow water but will often catch insects in flight. It is one of the most colourful and entertaining birds to watch. The bird most associated with waterfalls is the dipper (see waterfall number 115). It is unmistakable with its white front and bobbing action on a midstream rock. It is territorial and only seen singly or in pairs and always close to water. It feeds on benthic larvae, shrimps and the like. It may dive or simply walk into the stream and continue to walk along the stream bed hunting for its food. It is insulated from cold by air trapped in its feathers and would bob up to the surface like a cork but for the firm grip it keeps on stones on the stream bed with its powerful long claws. It builds a nest from grass and moss often behind a waterfall where it is safe from predators. It will fly to and from the nest right through the curtain of falling water.

5.

Waterfalls in Art

Seven centuries before European artists considered landscape to be a suitable subject for painting there was already a sophisticated school of landscape art in China. Three artists in the 10th century AD, Kuan T'ung, Li Ch'eng and Fan K'uan laid the foundations of Chinese landscape painting which has influenced artists to the present day. Paintings in ink and light colour wash on silk or paper were usually tall and narrow, depicting with fine brush strokes precipitous mountains, long vertical waterfalls, forests, temples, bridges and small human and animal figures. Over the centuries other artists contributed their own individual styles, notably Wang Meng (14th century) whose paintings were even taller and narrower, T'ang Yin (16th century), Wang Hui (17th century) who used a variety of styles including small dots of ink and Tao Chi (17th century) who employed greater freedom of long brush strokes.

However, in Europe, landscape only became a principal subject for painting as late as the 17th century. Previously landscape, often rich with symbolism, formed the background to religious scenes and portraits. Two Dutch artists popularised landscape art which often depicted waterfalls. Allart van Everdingen (1621-1675) is said to have been ship-wrecked on the coast of Norway where he spent his time drawing the rocky coastline. He travelled extensively in Norway and Sweden painting rugged mountain scenes. He influenced his contemporary painter Jacob van Ruisdael (1628 or 9-1682), the most notable Dutch landscape artist of the late 17th century. Waterfalls featured in many of his paintings. He often depicted their power accentuated by stormy weather. Van Ruisdael had a profound influence on landscape artists in Britain. Claude Lorraine (1600/4/5-1682), a Frenchman working mainly in Italy, sketched directly from nature. As artists began painting out of doors, the scenes that were depicted could be identified with greater certainty.

The 18th century saw a flowering of British landscape art including watercolour painting. Among the better known artists were Philip James de Loutherbourg (1740-1812), Francis Towne (1740-1816), Thomas Hearne (1744-1817) and Francis Nicholson (1753-1844). Francis Towne's spare style has a modern resonance. Artists of the day were influenced by changing attitudes towards the natural world and new concepts of what constituted 'beauty'. Edmund Burke (1729-1797) published a treatise in 1756 entitled *A Philosophical Enquiry into the Origin of our Ideas of the Sublime and the Beautiful*. He stated that the Sublime should "excite pain or danger". His ideas drove artists to seek out mountains, waterfalls and ravines, investing them with menace and grandeur. The countryside must have been full of painters in search of such scenes. Thomas Hearne painted his companions, Sir George Beaumont and Joseph Farington, sketching Lodore Falls.

Another influential artistic movement of the 18th century was the 'Picturesque'. William Gilpin (1724-1804), a Cumbrian, published his ideas in two volumes entitled *Observations, relative chiefly to Picturesque Beauty, made in the year 1772 on Several Parts of England; particularly the Mountains, and Lakes of Cumberland and Westmorland.* His views appear artificial and restrictive today. He stressed his rules of composition and popularised the painting of ruined buildings. Artists carried a small, slightly convex mirror, a Claude Glass, in which to view and compose the scene, a role now taken over by the camera viewfinder.

The 19th century brought new artists with new ideas. Peter de Wint (1784-1849), although fond of placid rural scenes of Lincolnshire also painted waterfalls. John Sell Cotman (1782-1842) was a prolific painter of waterfalls, mainly in Wales. James Ward's (1769-1859) huge canvas of Gordale Scar, housed at the Tate British, accentuates the scale of the scene. The period was, however, dominated by the two greatest names in English landscape painting, John Constable (1776-1837) and J.M.W. Turner (1775-1851). Constable visited the Lake District and painted at least one identified waterfall (see table). Turner, on the other hand, painted numerous falls in his prodigious output. In England he painted waterfalls in the Lake District, Yorkshire Dales and Teesdale (see colour plate 1A). Although influenced by ideas of the Sublime and the Picturesque, he broke through their constraints. He filled his pictures with grandeur and evocative atmosphere.

The later 19th century saw the rise of the Romantic Movement led by John Ruskin (1819-1900) and the romantic poets. This brought an interest in classical themes expressed by the Pre-Raphaelites. Ruskin himself painted Gordale Scar in Yorkshire and St Nectan's waterfall in Cornwall. William Mellor (1851-1931) and Edmund 'Waterfall' Gill (1820-1894) both painted many scenes depicting waterfalls, Edmund Gill mainly in Wales and Scotland. On the other side of the Atlantic Frederick Edwin Church (1826-1900) achieved acclaim with his painting of Niagara Falls.

With the arrival of the 20th century there was a decline in interest in landscape painting and 'serious' artists turned to other themes. There were, however, notable exceptions. John Piper (1903-1992) painted Gordale Scar and falls in Easegill in Yorkshire. Artists as diverse as Paul Nash (1889-1946), James Dickson Innes (1887-1914), and the American, Arshile Gorky (1904- 1948) (See colour plate 1B) all brought their own interpretations to the waterfall theme. Throughout the country there are competent artists today still painting from nature and still finding inspiration in waterfalls.

Why paint a waterfall? Why not be content with a photograph? So often, the reality far surpasses what a photograph conveys and the photographs in this book are no exception. Ching Hao writing in the 10th century put his finger on the problem-"He who tries to transmit the spirit by the means of formal aspect and ends by merely obtaining the outward appearance, will produce a dead thing."

Waterfalls have rarely been incorporated into the built environment. A notable exception is the house *Falling Water* in Pennsylvania designed by Frank Lloyd Wright (1869-1959). The house projects over the waterfall in cantilevered layers mimicking the rock strata over which the water cascades.

In the Ruskin Museum at Coniston can be seen a sculpture by Chris Brammall entitled *Lovely rock scenery, chased with silver waterfalls*. Vertical strips of stone, copper, silver, wood and steel evoke the scenes in the surrounding hills. Artists have placed their sculptures at waterfalls. An example is Alannah Robin's *Bean an t-Visce (Woman of the water)* in Grisedale Forest in the Lake District (see waterfall number 57). Isn't every garden waterfall and fountain a moving sculpture in celebration of falling water in nature?

Paintings and Watercolours of identified English waterfalls

Waterfall	Artist	Title of work	Where exhibited
Aysgarth Falls	George Cuitt (The Younger, 1779-1854)	Aysgarth Foss	not known
Aysgarth Falls	Peter de Wint (1784-1849)	Aysgarth, Yorkshire	not known
Aysgarth Falls	James Orrock (1829-1913)	Aysgarth, Yorkshire	not known
Aysgarth Falls	Philip Wilson Steer (1860-1942)	The Falls of Aysgarth near Richmond	Bolton Art Gallery
Aysgarth Falls	J. M. W. Turner (1775-1821)	Aysgarth Force	North Yorkshire County Library
Aysgill Force	William Hamilton (1751-1801)	Cascade at Gayle, Wensleydale	City of Birmingham Museum and Art Gallery
Aysgill Force	Francis Nicholson (1753-1844)	Ayrsgill Force, Wensleydale	Bradford Art Gallery
Catrigg Force	William Mellor (1851-1931)	Upper Catrigg Force, near Stainforth	not known
Colwith Force	Edward Lear (1812-1888)	Colwith Force, Langdale	not known
Dungeon Ghyll	J. M. W. Turner (1775-1821)	Dungeon Gill	not known
Easegill Falls	John Piper (1903-1992)	Easegill, a Yorkshire limestone chasm	not known
Easegill Falls	John Piper (1903-1992)	Limestone ravine, Easegill	not known
Fisherplace Gill Falls	Francis Towne (1740-1816)	In the Vale of St John, Cumberland, cottages at the foot of a waterfall	not known
Gordale Scar	David Cox The Elder (1783-1859)	Gordale Scar near Settle	Bacon Collection

Gordale Scar	Antony T. Devis (1729-1817)	The waterfall at Gordale Scar	not known
Gordale Scar	Antony T. Devis (1729-1817)	Gordale Scar, Mallam	not known
Gordale Scar	Thomas Girtin (1775-1802)	Gordale Scar, Yorkshire	The British Museum
Gordale Scar	John William Inchbold (1830-1888)	Gordale Scar, Yorkshire	not known
Gordale Scar	Francis Nicholson (1753-1844)	?Title	Whitworth Art Gallery, Manchester
Gordale Scar	John Piper (1903-1992)	?Title	not known
Gordale Scar	John Ruskin (1819-1900)	Gordale Scar: "from above like Bresson"	not known
Gordale Scar	J. M. W. Turner (1775-1821)	Gordale Scar	not known
Gordale Scar	James Ward (1769-1859)	Gordale Scar	Tate British
Hardraw Force	John Glover (1767-1849)	Hardrow Force, North Yorkshire	not known
Hardraw Force	Philip Wilson Steer (1860-1942)	Hardraw Scar	not known
Hardraw Force	J. M. W. Turner (1775-1821)	Hardraw Fall	FitzWilliam Museum, Cambridge
High Force, Teesdale	George Cuitt The Elder (1743-1788)	High Force	Private Collection
High Force, Teesdale	William Mellor (1851-1931)	High Force, Teesdale	Private Collection
High Force, Teesdale	William Mellor (1851-1931)	High Force, Teesdale, near Middleton	not known
High Force, Teesdale	Francis Nicholson (1753-1844)	High Force, Teesdale	Private Collection
High Force, Teesdale	John Brandon Smith (1848-1884)	Rise of the Tees, Durham	not known
High Force, Teesdale	J. M. W. Turner (1775-1821)	High Force	Yale Centre for British Art. Paul Mellon Collection
High Force, Teesdale	J. M. W. Turner (1775-1821)	High Force: Fall of the Tees	Art Gallery of New South Wales
High Force, Teesdale	J. M. W. Turner (1775-1821)	Fall of the Tees	Private Collection
Janet's Foss	William Mellor (1851-1931)	Janet's Foss near Malham	not known
Lodore Falls	George Beamont (1753-1827)	Waterfall at Keswick	Tate British
Lodore Falls	John Robert Cozens (1752-1799)	The waterfall of Lodore, Westmorland	Private Collection

Lodore Falls	Joseph Farington (1747-1821)	No title	not known
Lodore Falls	Thomas Hearne (1744-1817)	Sir George Beaumont and Joseph Farrington sketching Lodore Waterfall	Wordsworth Trust, Cumbria
Lodore Falls	Thomas Hearne (1744-1817)	View of Lodore Waterfall and Mill	Eton College Collection
Lodore Falls	Thomas Sunderland (1744-1828)	Cataract of Lodore	Fine Art Society
Lodore Falls	Francis Towne (1740-1816)	Keswick Lake looking toward Lodore Fall	Private Collection
Lodore Falls	Francis Towne (1740-1816)	Keswick Lake	Leeds Art Gallery
Mossdale Gill Falls	J. M. W. Turner (1775-1821)	Mossdale Fall (Near Hawes)	FitzWilliam Museum, Cambridge
Nunnery Walks Falls	Joseph Farington (1747-1821)	At Nunnery, Cumberland	not known
Nunnery Walks Falls	Joseph Farington (1747-1821)	Scene at Nunnery, Cumberland	not known
River Swale Falls, Richmond	George Cuitt The Elder (1743-1788)	The Foss at Richmond and Sleegill	Private Collection
River Swale Falls, Richmond	George Cuitt The Younger (1779-1854)	Falls on the River Swale at Richmond	Private Collection
River Swale Falls, Richmond	Peter de Wint (1784-1849)	A view of Richmond Castle in Yorkshire	not known
River Swale Falls, Richmond	Philip Wilson Steer (1860-1942)	Falls on River Swale at Richmond	not known
Rydal Lower Falls	George Barrett (The Elder)	View of a waterfall at Rydal	Courtauld Gallery
Rydal Lower Falls	William Mellor (1851-1931)	Lower Falls, Rydal Park, near Ambleside, Westmorland	not known
Rydal Lower Falls	Francis Nicholson (1753-1844)	Rydal Falls	Bradford Art Gallery
Rydal Lower Falls	Thomas Sunderland (1744-1828)	Lower Cascade at Rydal in the grounds of Sir Michael le Fleming Bart. Westmorland	not known
Rydal Lower Falls	Joseph Wright of Derby (1734-1797)	Rydal, Lower Fall	Derby Art Gallery
Rydal Upper Falls	William Mellor (1851-1931)	Upper Falls, Rydal Park, near Ambleside, Westmorland	not known

Rydal Upper Falls	Thomas Sunderland (1744-1828)	The Upper Cascade at Rydal in the grounds of Sir Michael le Fleming Bart. Westmorland	not known
Saint Nectan's Waterfall	Daniel Maclise (1806-1870)	Girl at St. Nectan's waterfall, Cornwall	Victoria and Albert Museum
Saint Nectan's Waterfall	John Ruskin (1819-1900)	Untitled	Birmingham City Art Museum
Scandale Beck Falls	William Mellor (1851-1931)	Falls on the Scandale	not known
Skelwith Force	Edward Lear (1812-1888)	Skelwith	Dalton Hall College, Preston
Skelwith Force	William Mellor (1851-1931)	Skelwith Force in flood, Westmorland	Private Collection
Skelwith Force	Thomas Smith of Derby (?-1767/9)	Skelwith Cascade	not known
Skelwith Force	Francis Towne (1740-1816)	Part of Elter Force, Westmorland	Private Collection
Stockghyll Force	Joseph Farington (1747-1821)	Ambleside Waterfall from the bottom	not known
Stockghyll Force	Joseph Farington (1747-1821)	No title	not known
Stockghyll Force	Thomas Sunderland (1744-1828)	Cascade above Ambleside	not known
Stockghyll Force	Francis Towne (1740-1816)	Waterfall near Ambleside	Oppe Collection, Tate Gallery
Stockghyll Force	Francis Towne (1740-1816)	A cascade near Ambleside	Private Collection
Stockghyll Force	Francis Towne (1740-1816)	A view from the cascade in the groves at Ambleside	Ashmolean Museum
Taylorgill Force	John Constable (1776-1837)	Sty Head Fall	Victoria and Albert Museum
Thornton Force	William Mellor (1851-1931)	Thornton Foss, Ingleton	not known
Thornton Force	William Mellor (1851-1931)	Thornton Foss, Ingleton	not known
Watersmeet Falls	John Brandon Smith (1848-1884)	The River Lynn, Devon	not known
Whitelady waterfall	Francis Towne (1740-1816)	A waterfall near Lydford	Oppe Collection, Tate Gallery
Whitelady waterfall	Francis Towne (1740-1816)	Lidford Waterfall	Oppe Collection, Tate Gallery

6.

Waterfalls in Poetry

Acceptable subject matter for poetry has changed with the years. Fashions come and go, but allegory has been employed by poets at all periods.

> With what deep murmurs through time's silent stealth
> Doth thy transparent, cool, and watery wealth
>> Here flowing fall,
>> And chide and call,
> As if his liquid loose retinue stayed
> Lingering, and were of this steep place afraid,
>> The common pass
>> Where, clear as glass,
>> All must descend
>> Not to an end;
> But quickened by this deep and rocky grave,
> Rise to a longer course more bright and brave.

These are the opening words of *The Waterfall* by Henry Vaughan (1622-1695) in which the waterfall is an allegory of death leading to resurrection. At that time aspects of nature, particularly symmetry and order were thought to reflect the nature of God, whereas the wild, unpredictable qualities were a consequence of the fall and the expulsion of Adam and Eve from the Garden of Eden. During the 17th century, nature held many terrors, both real and imaginary. Travel was hazardous. The wilder parts of the country were avoided by most people. Daniel Defoe described the Lake District as "all barren and wild, of no use or advantage to man or beast", and Exmoor as "a filthie barren waste". The 18th century saw a radical change. Nature began to be experienced and appreciated for itself. Ideas of the Sublime and the Picturesque (see Waterfalls in Art) were followed by the Romantic movement in poetry led by Wordsworth, Coleridge and Southey. No longer was nature full of hidden menace, nor was it there merely to be tamed and controlled, but its beauty and its grandeur could be enjoyed by all. Wordsworth (1770-1850) expressed his view of nature in *Lines composed a Few Miles above Tintern Abbey* which was included in the influential *Lyrical Ballads* by Coleridge and Wordsworth published in 1798. Here are two short extracts.

> The sounding cataract
> Haunted me like a passion: the tall rock,
> The mountain, and the deep and gloomy wood,
> Their colours and their forms, were then to me
> An appetite; a feeling and a love,
> That had no need of a remoter charm,
> By thought supplied, nor any interest
> Unborrowed from the eye. – That time is past,

And all its aching joys are now no more,
And all its dizzy raptures. - - - -
     - - - - For I have learned
To look on nature, not as in the hour
Of thoughtless youth; but hearing oftentimes
The still, sad music of humanity,
Nor harsh nor grating, though with ample power
To chasten and subdue.

By the 19th century, some were beginning to realise that the natural world was vulnerable and its beauty could be destroyed. This impassioned plea from Gerard Manley Hopkins (1844-1889) has a modern ring to it.

Inversnaid

This darksome burn, horseback brown,
His rollrock highroad roaring down,
In coop and in comb the fleece of his foam
Flutes and low to the lake falls home.

A windpuff-bonnet of fáwn-fróth
Turns and twindles over the broth
Of a pool so pitchblack, féll-frówning,
It rounds and rounds Despair to drowning.

Degged with dew, dappled with dew
Are the groins of the braes that the brook treads through,
Wiry heathpacks, flitches of fern,
And the beadbonny ash that sits over the burn.

What would the world be, once bereft
Of wet and wilderness? Let them be left,
O let them be left, wildness and wet;
Long live the weeds and the wilderness yet.

The 20th century saw poets still viewing nature through romantic eyes, still drawing allegories, but approaching their subject from new angles. Norman Nicholson (1914 -1987) was a poet who described the life and scenery of his beloved Lake District. In his poem *Beck,* he translates geology into poetry. Here are the opening lines.

Not the beck only,
Not just the water –
The stones flow also,
Slow
As continental drift,
As the growth of coral,
As the climb of a stalagmite.
Motionless to the eye,
Wide cataracts of rock
Pour off the fellside,
Throw up a spume
Of gravel and scree
To eddy and sink
In the blink of a lifetime.

A mother's view is expressed in *Behind the Waterfall* by Hilary Llewellyn-Williams (1951 –). The image through the waterfall illustrates the relationship between parent and her adolescent children. Here are the opening and closing lines.

> The waterfall is at its best today:
> Satisfyingly huge, it booms from its rock wall
> in a curve of white sound –
> an upturned river, fat with rain
> dense with crushed water, a sideways pull
> that draws the whole world.
> Up close, you can feel a wet gale
> sucking you in, tugging at the trees
> whose branches dance away
> and my children clamber and call.
> I don't worry, they're big now, this is their
> place, behind the waterfall
> while motherly I stand here
> on solid rock, to be someone to wave at
> to witness their daring.
>
> The waterfall roars between them and me.
> Fluid, unbreakable, a closed gate
> of running glass through which
> they waver and stand
> beyond reach yet visible, mouthing
> excitedly, deafened by sound
> of waterforms changing, exploding
> escaping, unstoppable, sweeping us all
> before it, downstream. And when, surprisingly
> they return, shaking the thunder from their brains,
> soaked through and laughing, it's like meeting
> again after a journey, after a dream.

For the sheer fun of river life *Gray Wagtail* by Norman MacCaig (1910 - 1996) takes some beating:

> It must be summer – you're wearing
> your black gorget
> above your sulphury shirt front.
>
> You dip and dip and go on dipping
> your tail, then shuttlecock up
> (death to a fly)
> and parachute down again
> on to your watery stone.
> It's necklaced with bubbles.
>
> No gossip you. You're too busy
> dip-dip-dipping your tail – ah,
> you're off
> in four looping, airy bounds,
> hurdling nothing,

to another watery stone
that wears a Beau Brummel jabot of foam
at its throat.

But you put it to shame, little dude.
You're the eight-inch spectacular
in the summery river's
fashion show.

Northumberland, North Pennines and Upper Eden Valley

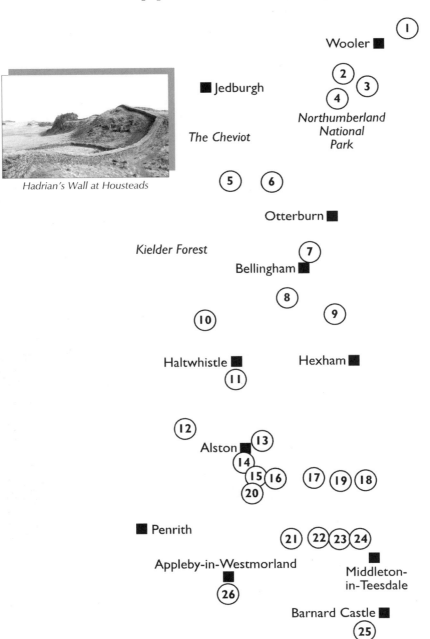

Hadrian's Wall at Houusteads

1   ROUTIN LINN

Berwick District, Northumberland

Maps: OS Landranger 75, OS Explorer 340.

Grid Ref: NT 983367.

Nearest towns: Wooler 9 miles (14 km), Berwick-upon-Tweed 12 miles (19km).

Walk: Grade – Moderate. Time – 8 mins each way.

Orientation: South-west.

The Falls: This splendid woodland waterfall takes a lot of beating. The water falls unbroken for about 9 metres on the right side of the fall. Most of the fall is arrested by a shelf of rock running obliquely down from left to right across the face of the fall. Some water splashes over and some runs along the shelf to the right side and into a large pool. The surrounding cliffs of gently dipping beds of sandstone are undermined at the level of the pool and contain a small cave on the left beside the path. All around are woods of oak and beech carpeted with bluebells in the Spring.

Access: Turn east off the A697 Morpeth to Coldstream road 5 miles (8 km) north of Wooler and just south of Milfield. Continue straight along this minor road for 4 miles (6km). Park on the grass beside the road where a road joins from the right and a footpath from the left. Walk along this track for 100 metres crossing a small stream with a waterfall. Look for a small path on the left leading off through the bluebell woods. Follow it down and round a promontory to the base of the falls.

2   # HARTHOPE LINN   ☆☆☆

Cheviot Hills, Northumberland

Maps: OS Landranger 75, OS Explorer OL Map 16.

Grid Ref: NT 927202

Nearest towns: Wooler 5 miles (8km), Morpeth 36 miles (58km).

Walk: Grade – Moderate. Time – 55 mins each way.

Orientation: North-east.

The Falls: These falls are hidden in a small but precipitous gorge and have to be sought out. Harthope Burn falls in a series of small cascades then drops six metres as one jet into a round pool before continuing down the gorge. The rock here is granite with a pink hue. This is a place to find seclusion far from the madding crowd.

Access: From the town of Wooler on the A697 road from Morpeth to Coldstream take a minor road south signed to Harthope Valley and Earle. Between Walkerwalls and Middleton Hall, turn right towards Langleeford. The road is steep up and then down. The road runs alongside Harthope Burn. Park where it becomes a private road. Walk on along the road past Langleeford Farm where it becomes a stony track. After Langleeford Hope it narrows to a footpath. Just after some sheep pens, take the higher of two paths then go obliquely down to the left to a wooded gorge to find the falls.

View from the waterfall

Granite in the Cheviots:
The granite rock seen here was intruded beneath the centre of the Cheviot volcano. Overlying lavas and tuffs which may have reached a depth of 1000 metres have been eroded away to reveal the granite in the central area of the Cheviot Hills. The Cheviot summit is just 2 km west of Harthope Linn.

3   LINHOPE SPOUT   ☆☆☆☆

Cheviot Hills, Northumberland

Maps: OS Landranger 81, OS Explorer OL Map 16.

Grid Ref: NT 958172.

Nearest towns: Alnwick 16 miles (26km), Morpeth 29 miles (46km).

Walk: Grade – Easy. Time – 35 mins each way.

Orientation: East

The Falls: Here Linhope Burn drops from heather and bracken moorland down into a wooded valley. The top of the falls is composed of a dyke of igneous rock forming well-jointed columns. Between two blocks of this rock, the burn drops in one unbroken jet into a deep pool. The pool is nearly closed off by a promontory, which forces the stream to make an S-bend into another pool. Beside the falls is a flat grassy area ideal for picnics. The falls are overhung with birch and willow. These falls are justifiably popular and are ideal for family outings. (Black Linn, which is shown on maps a short way downstream, is on private land and cannot be seen.)

Access: Turn off the A697 8 miles (13km) south of Wooler, 23 miles (37km) north of Morpeth, onto a minor road leading west and signed to Brandon, Ingram and Linhope. Continue through the Breamish valley and park by the roadside at Hartside Farm. Follow the well-signposted path to Linhope (pronounced 'Linnup') Spout.

Local history: Visit the informative Northumberland National Park Centre in Ingram. Here you can learn about walks in the Breamish Valley to suit all ages and interests, details of ancient hill forts and Roman remains in the area and much else besides.

4   DAVIDSON'S LINN   ☆☆☆☆

Cheviot Hills, Northumberland

Maps: OS Landranger 80, OS Explorer OL Map 16.

Grid Ref: NT 884157.

Nearest Towns: Alnwick 27 miles (43km), Morpeth 30 miles (48km).

Walk: Grade – Strenuous. Time – 2 hours 20 mins each way.

Orientation: South-west.

The Falls: These falls are well worth the trek. Usway Burn divides around a rocky island with a vertical downstream cliff. The larger left stream runs down a wide channel then drops vertically into a large pool. The attractive, smaller right stream drops in multiple falls to join the same pool. The Cheviot Hills contain the remnants of a huge volcano active in the early Devonian period 400 million years ago. The rocks at Davidson's Linn are volcanic basaltic lava.

Access: Park at Wedder Leap car park in Upper Coquet Dale (NT 866103). Walk up the road, over a stream, then back along the bridleway signed Middle and Border Ridge. At the farm, double back left up the hill, follow the track to a gravel road at the head of Murder Clough, and turn right. Within sight of Uswayford Farm, bear left into the forest. Follow this track using a large scale map, and turn along a very rough muddy track to the top of the falls.

Who was Rory? Look out for attractive circular sheepfolds. Some stream beds are full of mimulus (monkey flower, an introduction from North America), forming ribbons of bright yellow. Rory's still can be found in a small side valley downstream of the falls. Rory was a highlander controlling many illicit stills. He was renowned for his ruthlessness. To 'Rory' a sheepdog is to train it by fear rather than encouragement.

5   CHATTLEHOPE SPOUT   ☆☆☆☆

Redesdale Forest, Northumberland

Maps: OS Landranger 80, OS Explorer OL Map 16.

Grid Ref: NT 712010.

Nearest towns: Bellingham 18 miles (29km), Newcastle 42 miles (67km).

Walk: Grade – Strenuous, Time – 1½ hours each way.

Orientation: North.

The Falls: Chattlehope Burn exhibits two fine falls in quick succession. The lower is a fan-type fall about 10 metres high with a vertical drop at its base. The upstream one has a vertical drop of about 7 metres, broken and stepped towards its base. The fall is flanked by massive sandstone blocks and further angular boulders litter the valley floor below the falls. Not even the flies and midges in late August could detract from the superb view northward to the Cheviot Hills.

Access: Park in a lay-by on the A68(T) about 300 metres east of Catcleugh Reservoir. Toilets are provided. Walk west along the road, cross the dam and turn right passing below Chattlehope Farm. After climbing a stile into pasture bear left uphill and join a farm track. Follow it to its termination where a board shows the Chattlehope Spout Trail. Do *not* cross the footbridge, but follow the posted trail up the right bank of the burn. Having reached the lower fall, cross to the left bank by a footbridge and climb up to the upper fall. Do not attempt the right bank. Return by the same route.

Adders: On the track and path to the falls I saw two adders, widely separated, soaking up the summer sunshine. I mentioned this to the farmer's wife at Chattlehope Farm and she was not a bit surprised. The drawing is from a photograph of one of them.

See colour plate 2A

6 HINDHOPE LINN ☆☆☆

Redesdale Forest, Northumberland

Maps: OS Landranger 80, OS Explorer OL Map 42.

Grid Ref: NY 781999

Nearest towns: Bellingham 16 miles (25km), Newcastle-upon-Tyne 40 miles (65km).

Walk: Grade – Easy (steps may be slippery), Time – 15 mins each way.

Orientation: North-east.

The Falls: The falls nestle in a valley in Redesdale Forest floored with mixed woodland. The peaty Hindhope Burn falls over a 6 metre cliff of dark igneous tuff thrown up from an ancient volcano. The plunge-pool is bounded by angular boulders and lush ferns and trailing branches of honey-suckle hang beside the falls. By the footbridge below the falls, the burn drops over a huge wedge of rock shaped like a giant slice of cheese.

Access: Three miles east of Catcleugh Reservoir dam turn off the A68(T) Corbridge to Jedburgh road along a minor road signed to Forest Drive, Kielder Water and Kielder Castle. Park at a picnic area with adjacent toilets. Walk over a bridge following signs to Hindhope Linn Trail. The path is provided with strategically placed seats. Fifteen minutes will reach the falls, the round trip takes forty minutes.

The Rievers: Following the defeat of the Scots at the Battle of Flodden in 1513 and throughout the rest of the 16th century there were numerous cross-border raids by the Rievers. Bastles and pele towers, built for defence, provided some protection for the farming community. A few miles up the A68(T) near Carter Bar is the site of a famous battle, the Raid of the Redeswire (1576). On certain truce days the two sides met in peace to conduct business. The 7th July 1576 was one such day, but on this occasion tempers flared and a battle ensued.

Alas! That day I'll ne'er forget!
Was sure sae feard, and then sae faine -
They came theare justice for to gett,
Will never green to come again.

7 # HARESHAW LINN ☆☆☆☆

Bellingham, Northumberland

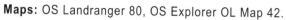

Maps: OS Landranger 80, OS Explorer OL Map 42.

Grid Ref: NY 842855

Nearest towns: Falls are at Bellingham, Hexham 16 miles (25km).

Walk: Grade – Moderate, Time – 40 mins each way.

Orientation: South.

The Falls: Although these falls are an easy walk from Bellingham, and are a popular tourist attraction, you feel when there that you could be many miles from civilisation. They are set in an awesome canyon of 100ft high, overhanging sandstone cliffs at the head of a wooded valley. The water falls obliquely for 10 metres across a black rock face into a large pool. Flat rocks round the pool allow close access unless the water level is high. There are stands of giant bell flower as well as wild raspberries, betony and wood avens.

Access: Hareshaw Linn is signed in the centre of Bellingham. The way leads to a car park on the east of the town from where a clearly defined path leads up the valley to the waterfall. The path was partly cobbled towards the end of the 19th century. Attractive small falls are passed en route.

Giant bell-flower

8 WARK BURN TRIBUTARY FALLS ☆☆☆

Wark Forest, Northumberland

Maps: OS Landranger 86 and 87, OS Explorer OL Map 43.

Grid Ref: NY 791759.

Nearest towns: Bellingham 10 miles (17km), Hexham 17 miles (26km).

Walk: Grade – Moderate. Time – 8 mins each way.

Orientation: North-west.

The Falls: Where Wark Burn emerges from Wark Forest a large tributary runs in from the right. Just before the confluence are these fine falls. The burn drops a little, is squeezed between sandstone buttresses, falls again and then finally drops 4 metres vertically into its plunge pool. There is sufficient water for the roar of these falls to be heard at a distance and the power in the churning water creates a strong impression. Heather covers the right bank while a solitary tree clings to the left.

Access: The B6320 road from Hexham to Bellingham passes through the village of Wark. Here take a left turn along a minor road heading west to Stonehaugh. At Stonehaugh, there is a small car park, toilets and picnic area. There are walks from here through Wark Forest. Having parked, walk over the bridge to the part of the picnic area on the other side of the burn marked by three totem poles. (What brings them here?) Climb a stile over a wire fence and walk up the right bank of the burn to the falls.

9   CROOK BURN FALLS   ☆☆☆

Tynedale District, Northumberland

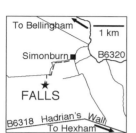

Maps: OS Landranger 87, OS Explorer OL Map 43.

Grid Ref: NY 863727.

Nearest towns: Bellingham 8 miles (13km), Hexham 9 miles (15km).

Walk: Grade – Moderate (muddy). Time – 20 mins each way.

Orientation: North-east.

The Falls: Between high sandstone cliffs, Crook Burn emerges from oak and beech woods. It drops over a small fall, runs horizontally then drops again about 3 metres over an outward curving rock shelf into a jumble of angular, moss-covered boulders. Along the edge of the cliff high above the falls stand a line of tall pines. Crook Burn is a substantial stream.

Access: Take the A6079 Hexham to Bellingham road. At a crossroads, turn left on the B6318 to cross the River North Tyne near the Roman fort and museum at Chesters. Turn right along the B6320 and after about 5 km turn left into the village of Simonburn, where there is a car park. From here walk on along the road, climbing a hill until you reach Tecket Farm. Climb a high stile on the left over a wall into a field. Cross the field keeping the farm on your left and enter another field that drops steeply down to the burn. Do not cross the burn by the footbridge, but turn right along the left bank of the burn to the falls which are at the corner of the field.

10   CRAMMEL LINN   ☆☆☆☆

Hadrian's Wall, Northumberland

Maps: OS Landranger 86, OS Explorer OL Map 43.

Grid Ref: NY 641697.

Nearest towns: Haltwhistle 8 miles (13km), Carlisle 20 miles (32km).

Walk: Grade – Moderate, Time – 10 mins each way.

Orientation: West.

The Falls: The best view of the falls is as they are approached. They are seen in their tree-lined valley surrounded by moorland. The River Irthing flows as two streams, which drop over numerous ledges into a large tranquil pool. The rocks here are Lower Carboniferous limestones, sandstones and shales. The different strata together with folding and faulting can be seen along this section of the River Irthing. The principal trees in the valley are rowan, ash, yew and silver birch.

Access: Three miles west of Haltwhistle leave the A69(T) for Greenhead. Drive on through Gilsland and along the road to Gilsland Spa Hotel. Continue along this road, turn right where the road ahead leads to Ministry of Defence property and park on the right where a footpath sign reads 'Permissive footpath to Crammel Linn and Gilsland Spa'. Walk down the path to the falls.

Hadrian's Wall: Crammel Linn is close to some of the most important and best preserved sections of Hadrian's Wall which is a World Heritage Site. Less than a mile west of Gilsland is the Roman Fort of Birdoswald, together with turret and milecastle. The visitor centre here is a good introduction to the wall and its history. Gilsland itself has a fine milecastle and a few miles to the east are the best preserved sections of the wall along its whole extent.

Hadrian's Wall at Cawfields

11   PARK BURN FALLS

South Tyne, Northumberland.

Maps: OS Landranger 86 and 87, OS Explorer OL Map 43.

Grid Ref: NY 700610.

Nearest towns: Haltwhistle 3 miles (5km), Hexham 18 miles (29km).

Walk: Grade – Moderate. Time – 30 mins each way.

Orientation: North-east.

The Falls: The Park Burn is a substantial river at this point. As it turns a right-angle bend, it breaks through a barrier of sandstone rock to fall as a segmented cascade into a large pool. There are fine cliffs both to the left of the falls and further upstream forming a backdrop to the falls. To the right of the plunge pool is a flat grassy area. Broom grows freely beside the falls.

Access: From Halwhistle take the minor road south past Bellister Castle and park by the telephone box at Featherstone Rowstock or 500 metres west in a car park. Walk back along the road towards Haltwhistle. Where it turns sharply to the left (north) and crosses the burn take a footpath to the right signed to Broom Houses and Linn Shields. Cross a pasture, turn up a bank, through a gate and on through Linn Shields Farm following the footpath signs. Bear right at a fork and continue high above the burn, which is on your right. Turn down when you reach the falls and not too soon.

Haunted castles: Nearby are two castles, Featherstone Castle and Bellister Castle, built in the time of the Rievers. Bellister can be seen from the road from Haltwhistle and is basically a ruined pele tower that has been extended to form a private house. Like so many old castles in this area, both are supposed to be haunted. Bellister Castle is visited by the Grey Man, a minstrel who was torn to pieces by a pack of hounds belonging to Lord Blenkinsopp, the owner of the castle. Featherstone sports a whole ghostly wedding party.

Bellister Castle

12   NEW WATER AND OLD WATER FALLS   ☆☆☆☆☆

King's Forest of Geltsdale, North Pennines

Maps: OS Landranger 86, OS Explorer OL Map 43.

Grid Ref: NY 617509, NY 604533

Nearest Towns: Carlisle 11 miles (18km), Haltwhistle 16 miles (26km).

Walk: Grade – Strenuous. Time – 2½ hours each way.

Orientation: West.

The Falls: The first falls encountered on Old Water are over blocks of dolerite. Butterwort flowers on the banks. Further upstream is a fine two-tiered perfectly symmetrical fall over flat sandstone ledges. On New Water, a ravine

One of the falls on Old Water

partially hides a powerful fall about 7 metres high. At the entrance to the ravine is an attractive fall over a dolerite intrusion about 10 metres high. Further upstream is a fine fall over sandstone ledges that clearly show cross-bedding and finally there are two more falls where two streams join in another ravine. In the floor of the ravine is a long block of sandstone worn smooth to resemble a whale's back.

Access: At Castle Carrock, about 4 miles south of Brampton, take the road signed to Geltsdale. Park beside the road at the end of a small wood on the right. Walk on along the road and branch left when the road becomes private. Cross a ford or footbridge below a house then turn left along a track leading onto the moor. At a T-junction turn left to Old Water Bridge and follow either of two tracks up the valley. Return to the T-junction and continue southward. When the track divides, take the left fork up to a higher contour line. The path is sometimes indistinct. Follow the contour and the falls will be seen down to the right.

Rocks: This is typical limestone karst scenery. The predominant rocks are sedimentary limestones and sandstones. A portion of the Great Whin Sill of dolerite crosses both valleys and forms some of the waterfalls.

13 RIVER NENT FALLS ☆☆☆

Alston, North Pennines

Maps: OS Landranger 86 and 87, OS Explorer OL Map 31.

Grid Ref: NY 724467 and NY 734468.

Nearest towns: Falls are at Alston, Penrith 19 miles (30km).

Walk: Grade – Moderate. Time – 35 mins each way.

Orientation: Both West.

The Falls: At Gossipgate Bridge the wide stream drops 2 metres over a limestone ledge producing a fall typical of limestone country and similar in form to many in the Yorkshire Dales such as Wain Wath Force. Unless the river is in spate, it falls through ten or so separate channels. Further upstream in a wood are falls of a totally different character. Here the rock is sandstone (still part of the Yoredale Series) and the river has carved a narrow channel through the rock and drops about 3 metres rebounding off numerous ledges as it falls into a large turbulent pool. The cliffs which curve away from the falls are undermined to some extent.

Access: Start from the centre of Alston. Walk down past the Turk's Head Inn into The Butts, a part of the town with narrow cobbled streets. Bear right past the Gossipgate Gallery to a bridleway signed to Corby Gates and Blagill. This runs along the left bank of the river to Gossipgate Bridge. Do not cross the bridge but continue upstream with the river on your left, climb several stiles and enter a wood to see the upper falls.

14   NATTRASS GILL FALLS   ☆☆☆

Alston, North Pennines

Maps: OS Landranger 86 and 87, OS Explorer OL Map 31.

Grid Ref: NY 719447.

Nearest towns: Falls are at Alston, Penrith 19 miles (30km).

Walk: Grade – Moderate. Time – 25 mins each way.

Orientation: West.

The Falls: These delightful falls are set in a deep wooded gorge with steeply sloping sides. They are crossed by a footbridge. The beck leaps gracefully from ledge to ledge down a six metre, nearly vertical rock face forming intricate patterns as it falls. At one point, the restraining fence has been broken by people climbing down to the foot of the falls. Be content with views of the fall from the footpath (unlike from where the photo was taken!) as the way down is very steep.

Access: Park in Alston. Walk south uphill and just before the main road turns left through Weardale to Durham bear right along a footpath signed to Nattrass Gill and High Nest. Follow this path, which is well sign-posted, all the way to the falls.

15   **THORTERGILL FORCE and**
SOUTH TYNE TRIBUTARY

Garrigill, North Pennines

Maps: OS Landranger 86 and 87, OS Explorer OL Map 31.

Grid Ref: NY 744422.

Nearest towns: Alston 3 miles (5km), Penrith 21 miles (34km).

Walk: Grade – Easy (not suitable for wheelchairs). Time – 4 mins.

Orientation: West.

The Falls: Garrigill Burn falls about 7 metres down a sandstone cliff bouncing off numerous ledges as it drops. The site is that of a previous lead and silver mine. While in the area visit a small, but attractive waterfall near Garrigill cemetery at NY 736423. This small burn runs straight down to join the River South Tyne.

Access: Thortergill Force is well signposted. Park in the car park or walk up from the village of Garrigill. A charge is made by the owners to see the falls, which are approached through the tea-rooms. For the other falls park beside Garrigill cemetery and follow the footpath slanting across one field, then continue across another field keeping a wall to your right until the falls are reached.

More at Thortergill:

At Thortergill, in addition to the waterfall, are a car park, tea-rooms that serve an enormous variety of teas and coffees and a forge where wrought-iron work can be purchased. Leaflets at the tea-rooms explain the history of the area.

16 ASHGILL FORCE ☆☆☆☆

Alston Moor, North Pennines

Maps: OS Landranger 86 and 87, OS Explorer OL Map 31.

Grid Ref: NY 758405.

Nearest towns: Alston 5 miles (8km), Penrith 23 miles (37km).

Walk: Grade – Moderate. Time – 10 mins each way.

Orientation: West.

The Falls: These are superb falls. Ashgill Beck drops 17 metres or so over a limestone cliff. The upper part of the cliff is a thick stratum of rock whereas the lower half is made up of thin layers. This lower part is softer and has eroded,

providing a marked overhang which throws the water 5 metres clear of the lower cliff face. A path crosses behind the falls. Framing the falls is the arch of the bridge carrying the B6277 road. The beck continues down a pretty wooded valley, with four more falls well worth visiting, before its waters empty into the River South Tyne.

Access: Park on the Alston side of Ashgill Bridge on the B6277 five miles south of Alston. Cross the bridge and take a footpath marked Ashgill. The first path branching off to the right leads to the falls through a narrow tunnel designed for the slim and agile. A second path on the right doubles back to the falls and is easier walking. To see the lower falls follow the path across a footbridge and down the right bank of the beck for about ten minutes.

Cataract: The medical term 'cataract', means an opacity of the lens of the eye producing cloudy vision and, in severe cases, blindness. The word is appropriate because sufferers from this condition view the world as from behind a waterfall. That is how the name arose.

17   KILLHOPE BURN and
SEDLING BURN FALLS

Weardale, North Pennines

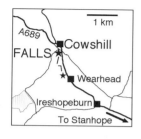

Maps: OS Landranger 87, OS Explorer OL Map 31.

Grid Ref: NY 855405.

Nearest towns: Alston 10 miles (16km), Stanhope 10 miles (16km).

Walk: Grade – Easy, but moderate to lower falls on Killhope Burn. Time – 2 mins to main falls, further 15 mins to lower falls one way.

Orientation: East.

The Falls: These are powerful falls as Killhope burn is more a river than a stream. The main falls are a scaled down version of High Force on the River Tees. The burn drops about 7 metres over the central part of a cliff composed of thick beds of sedimentary rock. The falls are framed by a fine two-arched stone bridge. The view may be somewhat obscured when trees are in leaf. Further down Killhope Burn are two attractive low falls. In the village of Cowshill, Sedling Burn joins Killhope Burn from the left. Two falls can be seen from the main road bridge and from a short foot-path down from this bridge.

Access: In Cowshill on the A689 ten miles west of Stanhope turn left down a road signed to Burtreeford and park a few metres down on the left. Walk on and cross the bridge and immediately turn left onto a footpath to view

the main falls. To see the lower falls continue along this path. Where the wall on your right turns right, bear left down to a gate and the path follows the burn to the lower falls.

18   ROOKHOPE BURN FALLS   ☆☆☆

Weardale, North Pennines

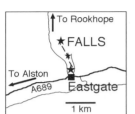

Maps: OS Landranger 91 and 92, OS Explorer OL Map 31.

Grid Ref: NY 953391, NY 948399.

Nearest towns: Wolsingham 9 miles (14km), Alston 18 miles (29km).

Walk: Grade – Easy to High Linn then moderate. Time – 5 mins to High Linn, further 20 mins to top fall one way.

Orientation: West and South.

The Falls: Rookhope Burn contains several impressive waterfalls. The furthest fall upstream, Turn Wheel Waterfall, is well worth the walk and is quite different from the others. The burn falls in multiple channels around blocks of dark rock. Water from the right of the falls then drops over a shelf at right-angles to the falls to link with the rest of the stream. Further downstream is a pleasing fall over a limestone shelf (illustrated). High Linn would be a fine fall without all the concrete at the top. Low Linn is best viewed from the side.

Access: Park in the village of Eastgate on the A689 5 km west of Stanhope. Walk up a road with a chapel on the left and church on the right. Just above the church turn left, follow a footpath, and cross the burn with a view of Low Linn from the bridge. High Linn is just a few metres upstream. Follow the path through a caravan site and on through woods to the upper falls.

Stanhope 'must sees': Durham Dales Centre in Stanhope 5 km east of Eastgate is well worth a visit. In the wall of the adjacent churchyard is set an enormous fossilised tree found in a nearby quarry. Stanhope Silver Band is justifiably famous and was founded in 1823.

19

MIDDLEHOPE BURN FALLS

Weardale, North Pennines.

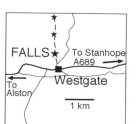

Maps: OS Landranger 91 and 92, OS Explorer OL Map 31.

Grid Ref: NY 906383, NY 905392.

Nearest towns: Wolsingham 12 miles (19km), Alston 15 miles (24 km).

Walk: Grade – Easy to first fall then moderate. Time – 10 mins to first fall, another 20 mins to top fall, both one way.

Orientation: South-west.

The Falls: The first fall to be seen is the most impressive of the lot. Here the burn is compressed between shoulders of rock and narrows further as it falls. The shape of these falls is similar to Skelwith Force in the Lake District. Just a few metres upstream are two fine falls close together where the burn is wide and falls over horizontal beds of limestone. Other falls are seen further upstream. Where there are old mine constructions look for a fall beneath a wide, turf-covered bridge. Finally, there are two horseshoe-shaped falls seen from the path high above the burn where there is a memorial seat.

Access: Park in a small car park on the south side of the River Wear at Westgate between Wolsingham and Alston on the A689. Walk back over the bridge and turn left along the main road and first right. Follow the third footpath sign on your left reading "Weardale Public Footpath. Middlehope Mine 1 mile". This path runs along the left bank of the burn past all the waterfalls.

Local mining: The rock along the valley is composed of beds of limestone separated by shales. All the beds were given names by miners e.g. Scar, Five Yard, Three Yard and Four Fathoms. They were mining for barytes for use, amongst other things, in the manufacture of paint. Many waterfall names in Northumberland end in 'hope' which simply means valley.

20   SOUTH TYNE FALLS   ☆☆☆

Near Garrigill, North Pennines

Maps: OS Landranger 91, OS Explorer OL Map 31.

Grid Ref: NY 760374.

Nearest towns: Alston 6 miles (10km), Penrith 22 miles (35km).

Walk: Grade – Easy with moderate scramble down. Time – 15 mins each way.

Orientation: North.

The Falls: The young river South Tyne falls by one or two streams about 6 metres into a pool almost completely surrounded by vertical cliffs. From this hidden pool, it escapes into a larger pool, tumbles over some rocks and then drops 3 metres into a third pool. A single tree guards this lowest pool. Further up the left bank are firs, pines and rowan. The whole complex pattern of falls, pools and cliffs is most attractive. The rock here is dolerite, another outcrop of the Great Whin Sill.

Access: South of Alston, drive through the picturesque village of Garrigill and continue south until the road becomes private. Park on the grass verge at this point. Continue on foot along the upper of two ways signed 'Public Bridleway to Knock.' After about 10 minutes walk, turn left to a stand of trees which marks the position of the falls.

21 CAULDRON SNOUT and MAIZEBECK FORCE

☆☆☆☆☆

Teesdale, North Pennines

Maps: OS Landranger 91 and 92, OS Explorer OL Map 19 and 31.

Grid Ref: NY 814286 and NY 802273.

Nearest towns: Alston 17 miles (27km), Barnard Castle 19 miles (30km).

Walk: Grade – Easy. Wheelchair access to top of falls. Moderate to Maizebeck Force. Time – 35 mins. Further 30 mins to Maizebeck Force, both one way.

Orientation: Cauldron Snout – South. Maizebeck Force – North-east.

The Falls: Cauldron Snout is England's most powerful series of cascades and is an awesome sight. The River Tees has been held back at Cow Green Reservoir. Now it is free to run its course, but meets the natural barrier of the Great Whin Sill, a complex intrusion of hard igneous rock responsible for many waterfalls. The river has smashed its way through this rock and drops 30 to 40 metres by four consecutive falls, the last one fanning out as the river reaches the valley below. Only if water levels are high should you follow the Pennine Way westwards to Maizebeck Force with its large pools.

Access: Turn off the B6277 Alston to Middleton-in-Teesdale road at Langdon Beck. Park at Wheelhead Sike car park on the east bank of Cow Green Reservoir. Walk along the road to the dam and then follow the Pennine Way footpath to the falls. A scramble leads down to the base of the falls.

The dam and the rocks: The building of the dam for Cow Green Reservoir has tamed this stretch of river. Gone are the severe spates of the past. Look for 'sugar limestone' on the banks of the reservoir. This is limestone that was subjected to intense heat (contact metamorphism) when the Great Whin Sill was intruded. Sugary is an accurate description of this rock.

22   BLEABECK FORCE

Teesdale, North Pennines

Maps: OS Landranger 91 and 92, OS Explorer OL Map 31.

Grid Ref: NY 874279.

Nearest towns: Barnard Castle 13 miles (21km), Alston 17 miles (27km).

Walk: Grade – Easy (not suitable for wheelchairs). Time – 45 mins each way.

Orientation: North-west.

The Falls: Blea Beck tumbles down a rocky hillside dividing as it falls into ever increasing strands as it bounces off innumerable ledges. Just below the falls, Blea Beck runs into the River Tees opposite a working quarry. Around the falls

are Juniper, Birch and a solitary Goat-Willow. Nearby are extensive 'forests' of mature Juniper, one of only three native British conifers, the other two being the Yew and the Scots Pine.

Access: See High Force (Fall number 24) and follow the route to view these falls from the right bank of the River Tees. Continue along the Pennine Way following the right bank of the river until Bleabeck Force is reached. If, and only if, water is running high go on to White Force by following the Pennine Way to a path junction and turn left. At the next junction, where there is a post and board, turn right to the falls.

The Pennine Way: Along the spine of England, from Edale in Derbyshire to Kirk Yetholm just across the Scottish border, the 270 miles of the Pennine Way afford some of the most arduous walking in the country. It was not Wainwright's favourite walk, possibly because it was wet and cold when he walked it. Much of it is certainly bleak, but who could complain of the stretch past Low Force, High Force, Bleabeck Force and Cauldron Snout?

23   **HIGH FORCE**

Teesdale, North Pennines

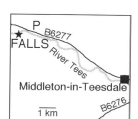

Maps: OS Landranger 91 and 92, OS Explorer OL Map 19 and 31.

Grid Ref: NY 880283.

Nearest towns: Barnard Castle 13 miles (21km), Alston 17 miles (27km).

Walk: Grade – Easy with wheelchair access. Time – 10 mins each way.

Orientation: North-east.

The Falls: These are England's most famous falls. No other waterfall can match it for its sheer power. Other falls may appeal by their delicacy and grace. Here the stark simplicity and ruggedness is reminiscent of a great Norman cathedral such as Durham which is not so far away. The roar of the falls is heard from a distance. The River Tees falls over a cliff composed of Whin Sill Dolerite resting on softer limestone. The black plunge pool is always choppy and foam-flecked. A flight of 75 steps lead up the left bank to the top of the falls and views down the gorge. Another fine view of the falls is from the Pennine Way footpath on the right bank of the river (see plate 2B). Here are orchids, wild mountain pansies and bog aspho-del.

Access: High Force is signed from miles away and from all directions. Park in the car park near High Force Hotel. A gravel path leads gently down to within sight of the falls, then a flight of steps down to the plunge pool. To see the falls from the right bank walk along the road towards Middleton-in-Teesdale till the pavement ends. Take a flight of steps down, cross the River Tees by a footbridge and follow the Pennine Way up the right bank to the falls. Look here for mountain pansies by the path.

See colour plate 2B

24   LOW FORCE and SUMMERHILL FORCE   ☆☆☆☆

Teesdale, North Pennines

Maps: OS Landranger 91 and 92, OS Explorer OL Map 31.

Grid Ref: NY 902281, NY 909286.

Nearest towns: Middleton-in-Teesdale 3 miles (5km), Barnard Castle 9 miles (15km).

Walk: Grade – Easy. Time – 5 mins to Low Force and 10 mins to Summerhill Force both one way.

Orientation: South-east and South-west.

The Falls: Low Force is a complex series of falls across the River Tees over an outcrop of the Great Whin Sill showing columnar jointing. An island support-

Low Force

ing larch and beech can be reached provided the river is not in spate. Facing the falls is a popular grassy picnic area. Summerhill Force could not be more different. Here Bowlee Beck falls over massive beds of sedimentary rock (limestone) with a marked overhang, known as Gibson's Cave, allowing access behind the fall. Other falls, worth seeing in their own right, are passed on the way up to Summerhill Force.

Access: Park at the car park near Bowlees Information Centre three miles west of Middleton-in-Teesdale on the B6277. Toilets are provided. Visit the Information Centre and shop. For Low Force cross the B6277 and follow the footpath signed to Wynch Bridge and Pennine Way. Summerhill Force is reached along a gravel path from Bowlees Information Centre or the car park signed to Gibson's Cave. There is no wheelchair access to either fall.

> **The historic Wynch Bridge:** *Just below Low Force is Wynch Bridge across the River Tees. This is a suspension footbridge built in 1830, a successor to the first suspension bridge in Europe which was built by lead miners in 1704 and collapsed in 1802.*

See colour plate 2C

25   HUGGILL FORCE   ☆☆☆

Teesdale, North Pennines

Maps: OS Landranger 92, OS Explorer OL Map 31.

Grid Ref: NY 976125.

Nearest towns: Barnard Castle 6 miles (10km), Appleby 22 miles (36km).

Walk: Grade – Moderate, Time – 10 mins each way.

Orientation: North.

The Falls: Huggill Sike forms a pattern of delicate tracery as it falls down a seven metre cliff, bouncing off ledges as it goes. The cliff and the sides of the ravine below the falls are composed of horizontal beds of sedimentary rock which vary greatly in colour and texture. A short distance below the falls the beck disappears underground unless it is in spate. In the ravine are scattered rowan trees, but not enough to obscure the falls.

Access: At the village of Bowes on the A66(T) south-west of Barnard Castle take the minor road south across the River Greta. Turn right at a T junction, cross two cattle-grids and park beside the road before a third cattle-grid. Take a bridleway on the right towards Bowes, but immediately strike left in a north-westerly direction to reach the ravine with the falls at its head. Enter the mouth of the ravine, where the approach is less steep, and follow the beck up to the falls.

26 RUTTER FORCE ☆☆☆

Upper Eden Valley

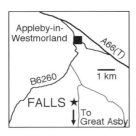

Maps: OS Landranger 91, OS Explorer OL Map 19.

Grid Ref: NY 682158.

Nearest towns: Appleby 3 miles (5km), M6 J38 13 miles (20km).

Walk: Grade – Easy. Wheelchair access. Time – 1 min.

Orientation: North.

The Falls: Situated in the beautiful Eden Valley this is a popular tourist attraction. The beck emerges from woodland to fall as a wide curtain which in spate shows its power to full effect. Here are a working waterwheel, ford and footbridge, art gallery and shop and a café.

Access: Take the B6260 south from Appleby-in-Westmorland. At the village of Burrells, bear left and follow the signs to Rutter Force. The falls can easily be seen from a car. They cannot be approached closely as they are on private land. When in spate wheelchair users should approach the falls from the west, turning off the B6260 at Hoff, about 1km south of Burrells.

The mill: The waterwheel is of the pitchback variety and is functional. The tailrace discharges into the beck just upstream of the wheel. At one time the mill was owned by the Great Asby Electric Light Company and generated electricity for the nearby village of Great Asby.

The Lake District

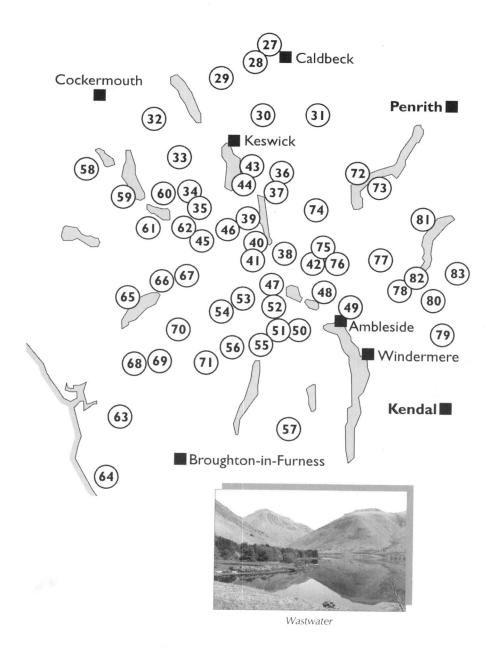

Wastwater

27   THE HOWK   ☆☆☆

Caldbeck, Lake District

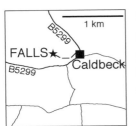

Maps: OS Landranger 90, OS Explorer OL Map 5.

Grid Ref: NY 318398.

Nearest towns: Carlisle 13 miles (21km), Keswick and Penrith 16 miles (25km).

Walk: Grade – Easy (muddy), Time – 8 mins each way.

Orientation: East.

The Falls: Here Whelpo Beck, a large beck or small river which becomes Cald Beck at the village of Caldbeck, flows through the only limestone gorge in the Lake District. Although the falls are not high (about 4 metres), they are impressive within the setting of the sheer-sided gorge. The main fall is split by a huge boulder. Further upstream is another smaller fall. The gorge is host to rare lime-loving plants including the Shield Fern. The valley is wooded mainly with oaks, sycamores and pines.

Access: There is a National Trust car park in the village of Caldbeck. From here walk upstream and follow a footpath signed 'Howk'. This leads past the preserved buildings of a previous bobbin mill to the falls.

Caldbeck attractions: Caldbeck has much to interest the visitor. The mill passed on the way to the falls was once powered by the largest waterwheel in the country, 3 feet wide and 42 feet in diameter. A traditional clog maker has his workshop in the village. Visit the Church of St Kentigern. St Kentigern was a Scot who preached to the people of Cumbria. He was affectionately and more commonly known as St Mungo. Hence St Mungo's Well near the river beside the church. In the churchyard is the grave of John Peel and his family. ("D'ye ken John Peel with his coat so gay?")

28   ROUGHTON GILL FALLS   ☆☆☆☆

Caldbeck Fells, Lake District

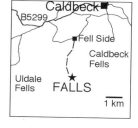

Maps: OS Landranger 90, OS Explorer OL Map 4.

Grid Ref: NY 302343.

Nearest towns: Keswick 15 miles (25km), Carlisle 15 miles (25km).

Walk: Grade – Easy, with a moderate scramble to finish. Time – 1 hour each way.

Orientation: North.

The Falls: (Not to be confused with Roughten Gill Falls). Altogether, this is a beautiful and varied series of falls. At the head of the gill, the beck is split by a large rock and plunges down the first fall. Then follow three falls shaded by rowan trees. At the lower end of the gill are two similar falls, one above the other, where the beck is squeezed between rocky buttresses to fall into dark pools.

Access: Park on the wide grass verge in Fell Side, two miles south-west of Caldbeck. Walk south towards the fells through a gate and turn right to follow the old mining track up the valley of Dale Beck until the spoil tips at the entrance to Roughton Gill are reached. Climb up the gill keeping the falls to your left.

Mining history: Roughton Gill mines, long since silent, were one of the richest of the Carrock Fells. Mining adits are seen along the sides of the gill. Skiddaw gives its name to the principal rocks of the area, the Skiddaw Series. These are ancient mudstones and sandstones laid down 500 million years ago in an ancient ocean, the Iapetus Ocean, long since disappeared. They were intruded, shortly after they were formed, by a variety of igneous rocks with accompanying rich veins of minerals. Lead, copper, zinc and manganese predominated, but no less than 23 minerals were extracted from Roughton Gill.

29   WHITEWATER DASH   ☆☆☆☆☆

Skiddaw, Lake District

Maps: OS Landranger 89 and 90, OS Explorer OL Map 4.

Grid Ref: NY 272313.

Nearest towns: Keswick 7 miles (11km), Carlisle 21 miles (34km).

Walk: Grade – Easy, moderate scramble at the end. Time – 50 mins each way.

Orientation: North-west.

The Falls: These falls were a favourite with Wainwright who wrote "for a grand succession of falls the first place must undoubtedly be given to Dash Falls". They are on a par with Forces Falls in Swindale and the falls in Fisherplace Gill, Thirlmere. They are seen from a distance and entice the walker onwards. From their base they look impressive as Dash Beck falls 20 metres or so in a shallow cleft with a few overhanging birch and rowan. Yet only half the falls can be seen from this point. There are further falls higher up and above them all the beck is crossed by a stone-arched bridge. There are fine views northward over lower lying farmland.

Access: Five miles north of Keswick turn right off the A591 road towards Orthwaite. After about two miles park beside the road near Peter House Farm. Take the tarmac track signed 'Bridle Path to the Falls, Skiddaw House and Threlkeld'. The surface changes to gravel, but the gradients are gentle. The looming mass of Dead Crags towers above and to the right. Take a narrow trod obliquely down to the foot of the falls. Return to the path and follow it to the bridge above the falls. From there, take another small trod down to view the upper part of the falls.

30   ROUGHTEN GILL and SINNEN GILL FALLS   ☆☆☆

Blencathra, Lake District

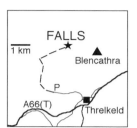

Maps: OS Landranger 90, OS Explorer OL Map 4.

Grid Ref: NY 309279 and NY 300282.

Nearest towns: Keswick 5 miles (8km), Penrith 15 miles (24km).

Walk: Grade – Moderate. Time – 1 hour each way.

Orientation: West.

The Falls: (Not to be confused with Roughton Gill Falls. Some maps actually spell this gill Roughton) The beck cascades down, turns left, then drops vertically within a narrow cleft, bouncing off ledges into a small round pool. Apart from two small rowans, the fell is treeless. The vegetation, however, is lush,

Falls in Sinnen Gill

particularly on the cliff face to the right of the falls. Here ferns, heather and mosses cling to the vertical rock. The small falls in Sinen Gill drop over large blocks of weathered, jointed granite.

Access: Park in the small car park at the Blencathra Centre in Threlkeld (NY 302257). Follow the track for about a mile with Glenderaterra Beck way below on the left. Cross the beck from Roughten Gill over a bridge made of huge stone slabs. They ring if they are tapped gently. Walk up the right bank of the beck to the falls. From here, walk north following the contour line to Sinen Gill. Note a sheepfold and follow the beck down to the fall. Walk south-west to the bridge that rings.

Local geology: The granite that underlies much of the Lake District reaches the surface at Sinen Gill, further north on the Caldbeck Fells, in Eskdale and at Shap. It was intruded in the early Devonian Period and heated the overlying mudstones and sandstones of the Skiddaw Series to produce a hard metamorphic rock termed 'hornfels'. The ringing slabs of the bridge are made of this rock, except for one which is foreign to the area and is a volcanic slate.

31 GLENDERAMACKIN FALLS ☆☆☆

Blencathra, Lake District

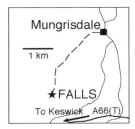

Maps: OS Landranger 90, OS Explorer OL Map 5.

Grid Ref: NY 346281.

Nearest towns: Keswick 10 miles (16km), Penrith 12 miles (19km).

Walk: Grade – Moderate (can be very wet). Time – 1 hour 10 mins each way.

Orientation: North-east.

The Falls: You have to keep your eyes skinned to find these falls, it is easy to walk past them. The River Glenderamackin must be crossed above or below the falls as they can only be seen from the right side and the path is on the left. The banks are steep and care is necessary. The water falls vertically in a single jet between cliffs into a deep, swirling plunge pool.

Access: Three kilometres north of the A66(T) Penrith to Keswick road on the east side of Blencathra is the attractive village of Mungrisdale. Park in the village. Take a footpath to the right of Bannerdale View cottage. A wooden footbridge beside a ford takes you across Bullfell Beck. At a fork, take the left branch following the left bank of the River Blencathra. The path is stony but can be very wet necessitating small detours. Cross Bannerdale Beck which may be tricky when it is in spate. Two miles (3 km) from Mungrisdale the path comes close to the river which is hidden in a ravine shaded by rowan trees. You have reached the falls.

32   SPOUT FORCE   ☆☆☆

Whinlatter Pass, Lake District

Maps: OS Landranger 89 and 90, OS Explorer OL Map 4.

Grid Ref: NY 182261.

Nearest towns: Cockermouth 4 miles (7km), Keswick 6 miles (10km).

Walk: Grade – Easy from Scawgill Bridge, Moderate from forestry car park. Time – 15 mins from bridge, 30 mins from car park return.

Orientation: South-west.

The Falls: These falls are seen from a viewing platform. Aiken Beck shoots over a 13 metre cliff of stratified Skiddaw 'slate' to drop into a plunge pool which is glimpsed through a cleft in the cliffs which almost encircle it. The beck flows on through a gorge in a plantation of spruce. Goldcrests and coal-tits can be seen and heard. There is no access to the foot of the falls.

Access: Drive from Braithwaite along the B5292 Whinlatter Pass road towards Cockermouth. Two miles after the Whinlatter Forest Park Visitor Centre there is a small forestry car park on the right and a sign "Walk to Spout Force". The path crosses two stiles then descends steeply down well-constructed steps. Cross the beck by a wooden bridge and turn right along the path from Scawgill Bridge to the viewing platform. At Scawgill Bridge there is space for three cars. This route avoids the steep steps.

Whinlatter Forest Park Visitor Centre: Here there are a shop, tea-room, toilets, exhibitions, children's play area, picnic area and a trail for wheelchair users. It is a popular venue throughout the year with something of interest for everyone.

33   LOW FORCE and HIGH FORCE   ☆☆☆

Bassenthwaite Lake, Lake District

Maps: OS Landranger 89 and 90, OS Explorer OL Map 4.

Grid Ref: NY 196215 and NY 192215.

Nearest towns: Keswick 3 miles (5km), Cockermouth 12 miles (19km).

Walk: Grade – Easy with wheelchair access to Low Force, Moderate to High Force. Time – 45 mins to Low Force, a further 30 mins to High Force both one way.

Orientation: East and south-east.

The Falls: These falls are remarkable in that one is an action replay of the other. The valley is blocked by Force Crag, down which Low Force tumbles. Above this point is a steep-sided glacial corrie with a similar crag divided in two by the white gash of High Force. The rocks here belong to the ancient Skiddaw Series.

Access: Either start in Braithwaite or park in a car park a short way up the hill from Braithwaite towards Whinlatter Pass. From here, a gravel track leads two miles up Coledale to Low Force. The track is well-compacted and has no steep gradients. This is a typical glaciated U-shaped valley. The meandering beck has begun to cut a V in the valley floor. A steeper stonier path leads up the right side of Force Crag to High Force.

Barytes mining: This whole valley is full of the evidence of a previous thriving mining industry with spoil heaps, adits and derelict mine buildings. Many minerals were mined here, the principal being barytes used in the manufacture of white paint. Some barytes deposits were exceptionally thick, up to 5 feet (1.5m).

34 SCOPE BECK FALLS ☆☆☆

Newlands Valley, Lake District

Maps: OS Landranger 89 and 90, OS Explorer OL Map 4.

Grid Ref: NY 214175.

Nearest towns: Keswick 5 miles (9km), Cockermouth 14 miles (22km).

Walk: Grade – Easy to base of falls then moderate. Time – 1 hour each way.

Orientation: North.

The Falls: Furthest upstream are pretty falls with a scissor action as the stream is thrown across by the rock wall on either side. It enters a pool from which it escapes over a projecting ledge of rock as a fan-shaped fall into another pool.

The lower falls are quite different being a long, narrow cascade hugging a cliff which overhangs on the right side.

Access: From Keswick drive south through Portinscale down into the Newlands Valley to the west of Derwent Water. Park at Chapel Bridge just west of Little Town. Walk over the bridge and turn left up the road past the little Newlands Church with its tiny school room tagged on to the end. It is no longer a school room, but a place for quiet and reflection – a dramatic change of use! Keep going past the cottages of Low High Snab. A grassy path leads up the valley past a small reservoir. Climb beyond the first falls to see the falls further upstream.

35   NEWLANDS BECK FALLS   ☆☆☆

Newlands Valley, Lake District

Maps: OS Landranger 89 and 90, OS Explorer OL Map 4.

Grid Ref: NY 229161.

Nearest towns: Keswick 6 miles (10km), Cockermouth 16 miles (26km).

Walk: From Rosthwaite. Grade – Strenuous. Time – 1½ hours each way.

Orientation: North.

The Falls: Newlands Beck runs an unlikely course. It drains the high land north of Honister pass then flows north in its own valley past Derwent Water and runs parallel to the River Derwent to open separately into Bassenthwaite Lake. As it drops from its source into its valley at Little Town it forms many waterfalls in attractive small ravines and clefts. One of the lowest is the most dramatic where it drops in a narrow jet about 16 metres into a small pool. Above and on either side are the huge crags of High Spy and Dale Head. Alchemilla and Parsley Fern grow in profusion.

Access: These falls can be reached from Little Town, Honister Pass or Rosthwaite. The restriction imposed by the Foot and Mouth epidemic meant I had to approach from Rosthwaite. The other routes would be less strenuous. From Rosthwaite car park walk westward through a farm to the bank of the River Derwent. Follow the river downstream, cross by a fine stone bridge and immediately turn left and within a few metres right over a stile and follow the right bank of a beck up Tongue Gill. Pass old quarries and at the top of the gill continue straight across rather boggy land to a path on the right bank of Newlands Beck. Follow it down to the falls.

Bridge over the River Derwent

36   MILL GILL FALLS   ☆☆☆

St John's in the Vale, Lake District

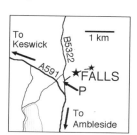

Map: OS Landranger 90, OS Explorer OL Map 5.

Grid Ref: NY 321198.

Nearest towns: Keswick 5 miles (8km), Ambleside 11 miles (18km).

Walk: Grade – Moderate but paddling if in spate, Time – 30 mins each way.

Orientation: West and North-west.

The Falls: Castle Rock towers overhead. Its north face is split by a great fissure from which the Mill Beck tumbles in a series of falls as if pouring straight out of the mountain. They are best seen from the right bank, which may necessitate a paddle to get across. The cliffs around these falls add a romantic dimension to the scene. The entrance to the fissure is graced with oak, holly, hazel and wild rose. Carefully climb the right bank and follow the gorge till it divides. Stand on a promontory and view fine waterfalls on the two contributory streams before they join and enter the gorge. Continue up the right bank of the right-hand stream (Mill Gill Beck) to see more falls further upstream.

Access: Park in Legburthwaite car park off the B5322 at the north end of Thirlmere. Opposite the toilet block take a path to the road, cross it and climb a stile. Immediately turn right along a track that goes up the hill. At a locked gate turn right, then across a stile between two huge boulders in a wall. Keep a wall to your left and the beck is soon reached.

Castlerigg Stone Circle: This stone circle is just 6 km to the north. It is one of the oldest and most beautiful stone circles in Britain. It is thought to date from the late Neolithic or early bronze age, 3000 years BC. Thirty-eight stones form a slightly irregular circle. Attached to the inside of the circle is a small rectangle of 10 stones. This arrangement is unique to Castlerigg. Further away is a solitary outlier. A single stone axe-head and some charcoal are all that have been found at the site. It is impressive at any time, but particularly in stormy weather!

37 FALLS IN FISHERPLACE GILL ☆☆☆☆☆

Thirlmere, Lake District

Maps: OS Landranger Sheet 9. OS Explorer OL Map 5.

Grid Ref: NY321183 NY324183.

Nearest towns: Keswick 6 miles (10km) Ambleside 10 miles (16km).

Walk: Grade of walk – Moderate (steep) Time of walk – 1 hour 10 mins each way.

Orientation: West.

The Falls: This is one of the finest series of waterfalls in the whole country. The beck that drains the northern slopes of Helvellyn drops in a series of nine falls: 1 – A fall into a narrow gorge overhung with juniper; 2 – A wide curtain of water is constricted down into a boiling pool; 3 – Just below 2 the stream drops twice through two pools; 4 – The beck crashes 40ft (12m) into a deep ravine concealing further falls; 5 – A single narrow spout; 6 – The beck launches itself into space over an unlikely triangular block of rock (see colour plate). On either side are jagged pinnacles. A single silver birch stands sentinel on the far bank. 7 – The beck thunders out of its gorge and widens out; 8 – Another single spout; 9 – A series of cascades in a more gentle wooded setting.

Access: Park in Swirls car park on the A591 near the north end of Thirlmere. Take the path signed Stanah and Helvellyn. Cross a beck and follow the path towards Stanah. Above Thirlspot Farm 30 metres after crossing a small beck and reaching a high fell wall bear right and cross the fell obliquely to the top of the falls in Fisherplace Gill, called Fisher Gill on some maps.

Painting: Back in the 18th century Francis Towne painted the buildings at Fisherplace backed by the fells and waterfalls. The painting, like others by the same artist, has a distinct modern style.

See colour plate 3A

38   # BIRKSIDE GILL FALLS   ☆☆☆

Thirlmere, Lake District

Maps: OS Landranger 90, OS Explorer OL Map 5.

Grid Ref: NY 328125.

Nearest towns: Ambleside 8 miles (12km), Keswick 9 miles (14km).

Walk: Grade – Easy (not suitable for wheelchairs). Time – 25 mins each way.

Orientation: West.

The Falls: A long ribbon of white water, visible from the main Ambleside to Keswick road, cascades down the fellside, breaking up into separate strands which reunite to separate again. At one point is a three-metre single vertical fall within the series. Occasional rowan, sycamore and Scots pine line the banks.

Access: Park in a car park behind Wythburn Church on the A591 near the southern tip of Thirlmere. Walk south along forestry paths through mixed coniferous woodland. Where the path emerges from the trees is a wooden footbridge at the base of the falls.

Red Squirrels: *Red squirrels may still be seen in parts of the Lake District including the woods beside Thirlmere. The threat of the grey squirrel is ever present.*

Red Squirrel

39   FALLS IN LAUNCHY GILL

Thirlmere, Lake District

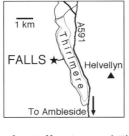

Maps: OS Landranger 90, OS Explorer OL Map 4 and 7.

Grid Ref: NY 307157.

Nearest towns: Keswick 7 miles (11km), Ambleside 9 miles (15km).

Walk: Grade – Moderate/Strenuous, Time – 30 mins each way.

Orientation: North and east.

The Falls: Around Thirlmere are several similar falls, but these are one of the best. Launchy Beck tumbles down a series of falls in a steep wooded ravine which is a Site of Special Scientific Interest owned by North-west Water. The path follows the right bank of the ravine. First encountered is a deep ravine with vertical walls. Just upstream are two falls. Further up is an impressive fall where the beck splits round a huge rock then reunites into a single fall. Further upstream still is the highest single vertical drop of the series. More falls are encountered as deciduous woods give place to conifers. There are fine views across Thirlmere.

Access: Follow the minor road along the west bank of Thirlmere and park in a lay-by about half way along the lake. A well-defined and signed path leads up the gill.

Lakes and reservoirs: What is it about reservoirs that makes them so different from natural lakes? In the Lake District both Thirlmere and Haweswater are reservoirs formed by the damming (damning?) of previously existing lakes to provide water for Manchester. Thirlmere appears to have mellowed somewhat with time and maybe in a century or two it will be indistinguishable from a natural lake.

40 DOB GILL FALLS ☆☆☆

Thirlmere, Lake District

Maps: OS Landranger 90, OS Explorer OL Map 5.

Grid Ref: NY 313132.

Nearest towns: Keswick 9 miles (14km), Ambleside 9 miles (14km).

Walk: Grade – Moderate. Time – 45 mins. each way.

Orientation: North and North-east.

Lower falls

The Falls: There are two separate sets of falls on Dob Gill Beck. The upper falls are in moorland with scattered silver birch. The beck tumbles down a series of falls into a small round pool and enters a narrow deep ravine with sheer walls. The lower falls are again a series of drops, this time in a plantation mainly of conifers. The falls are seen between the trunks of pine trees, which do not obscure the view.

Access: Park in Dobgill car park towards the southern end of Thirlmere on the minor road that runs along the west bank. Walk up a zigzag path through the woods for 15 mins to the lower falls. Continue up to a T-junction, turn left, cross the beck by a footbridge, go through a gate designed to keep out deer and immediately turn right along the edge of the plantation. Go through a gate or stile and turn right again until the stream is reached. Follow its right bank up to the falls.

Upper Falls

41 WYTH BURN FALLS ☆☆☆

Thirlmere, Lake District

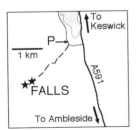

Maps: OS Landranger 90, OS Explorer OL Map 5.

Grid Ref: NY 308117 and NY 311118.

Nearest towns: Ambleside 8 miles (12km), Keswick 9 miles (15km).

Walk: Grade – Moderate. Time – 45 mins each way.

Orientation: East.

The Falls: The upper falls form a complex pattern of vertical drops, broken cascades and slides on the open fellside. The lower falls are similar, but here the beck is constricted by rocky walls on which cling three small rowan trees.

Lower Wyth Burn Falls seen through mist and light rain

Access: Park at Steel End car park on a minor road as it curls round the southern end of Thirlmere. Cross the road and take a footpath up the left bank of the beck. Cross by a footbridge to the right bank and continue up past a bend to the right to reach the falls.

42 TONGUE GILL FALLS ☆☆☆

Dunmail Raise, Lake District

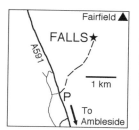

Maps: OS Landranger 90, OS Explorer OL Map 5.

Grid Ref: NY 348111.

Nearest towns: Ambleside 5 miles (8km), Keswick 12 miles (19km).

Walk: Grade – strenuous. Time – 1 hour each way.

Orientation: South-west.

The Falls: The upper part of these falls beckons you on from over a mile away. These are where Tongue Gill Beck spills out of Hause Moss, the marshy land between Seat Sandal and Fairfield. The beck appears over the skyline and spreads out over dark rock in a series of falls. It then gathers itself together and falls in a wide zigzag between a scattering of Rowan trees before being confined in a dramatic narrow cleft in the rock for a third series of falls. The views from these falls are magnificent.

Access: Dunmail Raise is the pass South of Thirlmere crossed by the A591 road from Ambleside to Keswick. Park beside this road at Mill Bridge 2 km north of the village of Grasmere. Take the footpath towards Patterdale, which passes between dry stone walls. The track climbs above the beck, which can be heard in the woods to the right. Cross Little Tongue Gill Beck by large stepping-stones and then over to the left bank of Tongue Gill Beck by a wooden footbridge. Take the well-defined path up the gill with the beck below you to the left. Where the gradient steepens the path is well constructed with laid stones and drainage channels. The path crosses to the right side of the beck just below the highest group of falls.

BARROW BECK FALLS

43

☆☆☆☆

Derwent Water, Lake District

Maps: OS Landranger 89 and 90, OS Explorer OL Map 4.

Grid Ref: NY 278193.

Nearest towns: Keswick 2 miles (3km), Penrith 20 miles (32km).

Walk: Grade – Moderate, with a steep scramble. Time – 30 mins each way.

Orientation: North-west.

The Falls: On the way up towards Ashness Gill there are several small falls with grassy areas ideal for picnics. One is overhung by two fine junipers. The head of the valley is blocked by a huge cliff over which two becks tumble and join at its foot. The more northerly falls carry less water and are partially hidden by trees. The larger, southerly beck which drains the north-western slopes of High Seat, falls almost vertically for 20 metres or so down a narrow cleft into a deep pool. There are fine views over Derwent Water and Bassenthwaite Lake to the Western Fells.

Access: Park in Strutta Wood car park by Ashness Bridge on the narrow road to Watendlath. Alternatively (and Strutta Wood car park may well be full) use one of the car parks on the Keswick to Borrowdale road and walk up to Ashness Bridge. Having taken the obligatory photo of the bridge, which must be the most photographed bridge in the Lake District, walk up the path along the left bank of Barrow Beck. The last 50 metres to the base of the falls involve a scramble over rocks, but this is not difficult.

44

LODORE FALLS

Derwent Water, Lake District

Maps: OS Landranger 89 and 90, OS Explorer OL Map 4.

Grid Ref: NY 265187.

Nearest towns: Keswick 3 miles (5km), Cockermouth 17 miles (27km).

Walk: Grade – Easy to base, strenuous to top. Time – 2 mins from hotel, 15 mins from car park. A further 15 mins to the top falls one way.

Orientation: South.

The Falls: These famous falls must be seen after rain otherwise they may disappoint. In spate, though, they are impressive. Watendlath Beck falls

between two towering cliffs, Shepherd's Crag and Gowder Crag, and down a boulder-choked ravine to empty into Derwent Water. At the head of this ravine, just before the beck turn sharply from west to south, are the upper falls which make as loud a roaring in spate as the lower falls.

Access: Patronise the Lodore Hotel or park in Kettlewell car park towards the southern end of Derwent Water and walk through the woods to the falls behind the hotel. A steep scramble up the right bank leads to the upper falls.

__The Romantics:__ These falls were beloved of the Romantic painters and poets. The force of the water in spate, the rocks and the crags together with the deafening roar of the falls, appealed to their sense of the awesomeness of nature. *The falls were popularised by Robert Southey's poem (doggerel?)* How does the water come down at Lodore? *Southey also wrote the story of the Three Bears and the first history of Brazil!*

45   SOUR MILK GILL and TAYLOR GILL FALLS ☆☆☆☆

Borrowdale, Lake District

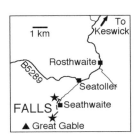

Maps: OS Landranger 89 and 90, OS Explorer OL Map 4.

Grid Ref: NY 230123 and NY 230110.

Nearest towns: Keswick 8 miles (13km), Cockermouth 17 miles (27km).

Walk: Grade – Moderate with scrambling. Time – Sour Milk Gill 30 mins, Taylor Gill 45 mins both one way.

Orientation: Both East.

The Falls: Viewed from the valley floor the beck appears to flow over a promontory of rock before dropping down Sour Milk Gill. There follows a series of falls of differing character. The highest is through a harsh landscape of jagged

Top of Sour Milk Gill.

pinnacles of rock. Lower down the beck fans out as multiple streams over a wide rock face (the sour milk effect) below which it drops into a pretty cleft overhung with silver birch and holly. There are fine views down Borrowdale to Skiddaw and Blencathra. Taylor Gill Falls is an impressive drop of about 25 metres into a plunge pool. Scree extends almost to the base of the falls. The scene is softened by a row of larch and pines above the falls silhouetted against the sky.

Access: Park at the roadside just before Seathwaite at the southern end of Borrowdale. Walk to Seathwaite farm (refreshments served in the Summer) and turn right under an arch in the farm buildings. Cross the River Derwent by a wooden footbridge. For Sour Milk Gill, continue straight ahead over a ladder stile to the falls. For Taylor Gill turn left along a footpath which follows the left bank of the River Derwent. The path swings right into Styhead Gill. To get close to the falls involves scrambling over rocks, passing through a rather surprising gate and descending down a scree slope.

The Weather: Seathwaite has the highest rainfall of any inhabited place in England – 140 inches a year. Let's hope you have a fine day for your visit. The approach to Borrowdale is through the Jaws of Borrowdale, a narrow gap in the hills south of Derwent Water. It is said that once upon a time the men of Borrowdale planned to build a high wall across the Jaws of Borrowdale to prevent the cuckoo flying away so that Borrowdale would enjoy perpetual Spring.

46   GALLENY FORCE and GREENUP GILL FALLS ☆☆☆

Borrowdale, Lake District

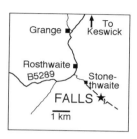

Maps: OS Landranger 89 and 90, OS Explorer OL Map 4.

Grid Ref: NY 273131 and NY 280122.

Nearest towns: Keswick 7 miles (11km), Cockermouth 17 miles (27km).

Walk: Grade – Moderate, Time – 25 mins to Galleny Force one way.

Orientation: South-west.

The Falls: Galleny Force is a powerful, though not high, waterfall where Stonethwaite Beck describes a Z bend in a delightful setting of grass, rocks and ancient gnarled trees. An ideal picnic spot. All around are other falls. Between Stonethwaite and Galleny Force, falls are seen tumbling down Willigrass Gill on one hand and Little Stanger Gill on the other. A 40-minute walk (one way) upstream leads to further falls in Greenup Gill. The furthest is at the confluence of two becks. Another is split by a large rock supporting a juniper and a silver birch. The walk up Greenup Gill is rewarding.

Access: In Borrowdale follow the signs to Stonethwaite and park there. The footpath beyond the inn leads up the valley to Galleny Force. To explore Greenup Gill follow the footpath a short way along Langstrath Beck which enters Stonethwaite Beck from the left. Cross Langstrath Beck by a footbridge and walk down its right bank through a gate and keep close to the water. Cross Stonethwaite Beck by a bridge just above the confluence with Langstrath Beck, turn right and walk up the right bank to Greenup Gill and its falls.

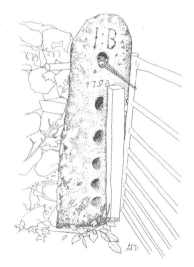

Stone gateposts: In Borrowdale there are many ancient stone gateposts. The five or six holes would once have taken wooden poles. Some of these posts are still used to support modern gates. Look for the initials of the owners carved into the posts.

47   SOURMILK GILL and BLINDTARN GILL FALLS   ☆☆☆

Easedale, Lake District

Maps: OS Landranger 90, OS Explorer OL Map 7.

Grid Ref: NY 318086 and NY 321080.

Nearest towns: Ambleside 4 miles (7km), Keswick 12 miles (20km).

Walk: Grade – Easy to base of falls then moderate. Time – 30 mins each way to either fall.

Orientation: South-east.

The Falls: At least three falls in the Lake District are called Sourmilk and look from a distance like milk pouring down the fell. The falls described here can be seen from a long way away. Easedale Beck leaves Easedale Tarn and drops between Brinhowe Crag and Ecton Crag in a string of cascades, but there are a few vertical drops. At one point, the beck divides round an attractive rocky island supporting rowan and juniper. There are fine views down Easedale to Grasmere. The energetic may wish to visit the falls in Blindtarn Gill where the beck drops 7 metres into a small pool in a secluded ravine.

Access: From Grasmere walk north-west along Easedale Road. Where it turns sharp right, take the footpath towards Easedale Tarn. After a couple of foot-bridges in a wood it follows the right bank of Easedale Beck to a gate where the path forks. The left branch leads to Blindtarn Falls, the right to Sourmilk Gill. Sourmilk Gill Falls are visible for most of the way. To reach Blindtarn Gill Falls bear left at the gate, past a cottage on your right and walk up the fell with the beck on your right. A steep walk down from the path brings you to the falls.

48 RYDAL FALLS ☆☆☆

Rydal Water, Lake District

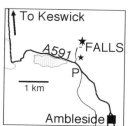

To Keswick

A591 *FALLS

P

1 km

Ambleside

Maps: OS Landranger 90, OS Explorer OL Map 7.

Grid Ref: NY 365068 and NY 365064.

Nearest towns: Ambleside 1 mile (2km), Keswick 15 miles (24km).

Walk: Grade – Moderate to upper falls, easy with wheelchair access to lower falls. Time – 8 mins to either falls.

Orientation: South-east.

The Falls: The upper falls are a single drop of about 6 metres. A large angular boulder is wedged between the cliffs at the top of the falls. When in spate the boulder is completely covered. Below these are more falls in the wooded valley full of beech trees. The lowest falls are at Rydal Hall and can be viewed from a bridge across its plunge pool.

Lower falls from the bridge.

Access: Walk from Ambleside or park on the left side of the road leading up from the A591 to Rydal Hall and Rydal Mount. There is also a car park on the west side of the A591 across Pelter Bridge. Walk up past Rydal Hall and Rydal Mount, the road becomes a stony track. Follow a footpath signed 'Access Area' and turn through a small gate on the right signed 'Birk Hagg Access Area by agreement with the Rydal Estate'. This steep path with steps descends to a footbridge and up the left bank to the upper falls. To see the lower falls enter the gardens of Rydal Hall which are open to the public all the year. There is a collecting box for contributions. Walk beneath the terraced gardens to a bridge to view the falls.

Wordsworth: *Rydal Mount was home to William Wordsworth from 1813 until he died there in 1850. His family still owns the property. The house contains furniture owned by Wordsworth, portraits, paintings and the poet's attic study. He designed the gardens which, together with the house, are open to the public. Wordsworth describes a waterfall in An Evening Walk which he identified as the lower falls at Rydal. Visit Dove Cottage just up the road at Grasmere and the house where Wordsworth was born in Cockermouth.*

49 STOCKGHYLL FORCE ☆☆☆☆

Ambleside, Lake District

Maps: OS Landranger 90, OS Explorer OL Map 7.

Grid Ref: NY 384046.

Nearest towns: At Ambleside, Penrith 22 miles (35km).

Walk: Grade – Easy (can be muddy). Time – 30 mins round trip.

Orientation: West.

The Falls: These are impressive woodland gorge waterfalls within easy walking distance of Ambleside. At the head of the falls, the beck divides into two and later the right branch divides again. The two left branches join above the longest drop and finally the beck reunites to continue its hectic course down the gill. The scene is enriched by the woodland setting with beech the predominant tree. There are several viewing points from the path around the falls.

Access: From the centre of Ambleside walk up the road behind Barclay's Bank and the Salutation Hotel and follow the signs to the waterfalls. Enter Stockghyll Park on the left and take the path along the left side of the beck. Do not cross the first footbridge, but continue up the left bank. Having viewed the falls cross the footbridge above the falls and return down the right bank.

Ambleside Architecture: *Ambleside is a fascinating town with many examples of Lakeland vernacular architecture. The tiny 17th century Bridge House (illustrated) was once home to a basket maker, his wife and six children! Follow the excellent Ambleside Heritage Trail published by Ambleside Civic Trust. Typical features of old domestic architecture are cylindrical chimneys, deep-set windows and overhanging eaves to protect from rain, and on a few old properties there are 'wrestler slates' along the ridges of the slate roofs.*

The Bridge House

50   SKELWITH FORCE   ☆☆☆

Windermere, Lake District

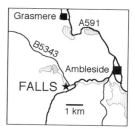

Maps: OS Landranger 90, OS Explorer OL Map 7.

Grid Ref: NY342034.

Nearest towns: Ambleside 2 miles (4km), Coniston 5 miles (8km).

Walk: Grade – Easy. Time – 5 mins each way.

Orientation: East.

The Falls: The River Brathay drains Elterwater which collects water from Great Langdale and Little Langdale. At Skelwith Force the river is squeezed between massive, flat topped rock buttresses. When in spate the power of the water is impressive. The rocks give easy access to the head and foot of the falls.

The valley of the Brathay is wooded with oak, beech, sycamore, hazel and rowan, but is wide enough to give the falls an open aspect and let in the sunlight (if you're lucky). Skelwith Force has been and still is a popular subject for artists.

Access: Park or take the bus to Skelwith Bridge at the bottom of the road to Elterwater. Walk up the road past a slate works and take a footpath into the woods towards Elterwater. The falls are quickly reached.

Beatrix Potter – much more than rabbits: *Beatrix Potter lived south of Skelwith at Sawrey. Her name is indelibly printed on the Lake District. She would be remembered for her children's books alone and their loveable characters: Peter Rabbit, Mrs Tiggywinkle, Jeremy Fisher and many others. Yet her influence in other fields was great. She bred Herdwick sheep and did much to popularise the breed in the Lake District. She was the first to catalogue the fungi of the British Isles and to show that lichens are algae and fungi in a symbiotic relationship. She was a champion for environmental protection before the phrase was coined and was a staunch supporter of the work of the National Trust in the Lake District. Her house at Sawrey is now a museum.*

51   COLWITH FORCE

Little Langdale, Lake District

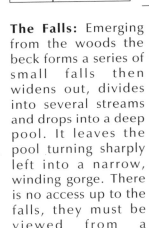

Maps: OS Landranger 90, OS Explorer OL Map 7.

Grid Ref: NY 328032.

Nearest towns: Ambleside 3 miles (5km), Coniston 4 miles (6 km).

Walk: Grade – Moderate. Time – 25 mins each way.

Orientation: South-east.

The Falls: Emerging from the woods the beck forms a series of small falls then widens out, divides into several streams and drops into a deep pool. It leaves the pool turning sharply left into a narrow, winding gorge. There is no access up to the falls, they must be viewed from a distance. All around is deciduous woodland, mainly oak.

Access: From Ambleside take the A593 road towards Coniston. Just over 1 km beyond Skelwith Bridge park in a lay-by where there is a post box. Walk on and turn right down a minor road signed to Elterwater. After a little less than 1 km, you reach Colwith Bridge where there may be parking for one or two cars. Enter woods on your left by either of two stiles. A National Trust sign points to Colwith Force. Climb up a stony path to reach a well-made gravel path that leads quickly to the falls.

52   MEGS GILL FALLS   ☆☆☆

Great Langdale, Lake District

Maps: OS Landranger 90, OS Explorer OL Map 7.

Grid Ref: NY 323059.

Nearest towns: Ambleside 4 miles (6km), Coniston 5 miles (8km).

Walk: Grade – Strenuous. Time – 45 mins each way.

Orientation: South-east.

The Falls: This is a fine series of linked cascades down the fellside; a smaller version of Cautley Spout. To get close to the water involves a steep scramble and the falls are better and more safely viewed from a distance. I had to climb down to retrieve my rucksack with camera that rolled down into the ravine. No harm done to them or me. At each turn of the falls are scattered rowan,

hawthorn, birch and juniper getting larger at lower altitude.

Access: Park in the car park off the B5343 at Elterwater and walk along the road to Chapel Stile. Parking is very limited at Chapel Stile and is best not attempted. Walk up past the church and a few houses. An unsigned path turns left up the fell. Follow this path steeply upwards beside a small beck and dry stone wall. Turn right when the wall turns right, but immediately turn left straight up the fell again. The path crosses the beck just above the falls. Continue for a few metres and turn round for the best view of the falls. The whole extent of the falls can be seen by continuing along the path, turning right along the ridge and looking back.

53 DUNGEON GHYLL FORCE and STICKLE GHYLL FALLS

☆☆☆☆

Great Langdale, Lake District

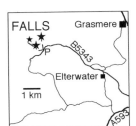

Maps: OS Landranger 89 and 90, OS Explorer OL Map 6.

Grid Ref: NY 288066 and NY 290071.

Nearest towns: Ambleside 6 miles (10km), Coniston 8 miles (13km).

Walk: Grade – Moderate. Time – 20 mins to Dungeon Ghyll, 35 mins to Stickle Ghyll, both one way.

Orientation: East and South-east.

The Falls: A deep vertically sided cleft, hardly wider than the beck itself, leads back to a tall narrow fall. The chasm is bridged at the head of the fall by two large blocks of stone. The floor is strewn with huge boulders. It is possible to scramble over these to approach the foot of the fall. It gives a sense of claustrophobia. Dungeon Ghyll is aptly named. Wainwright much preferred the falls in the ravine just above Dungeon Ghyll Force. Five minutes walk further up the fell reveals some more fine falls this time with an open aspect. Stickle Ghyll is well worth seeing. It contains a series of falls from open fell to a wooded ravine.

Access: Take the B5343 road from Skelwith Bridge into Great Langdale. Park in the car park near the New Dungeon Ghyll Hotel. Follow the foot path past the hotel, bear left through a gap in a wall, through a gate, turn right past a bench, over a stile and cross on convenient stones to the right side of the beck. Climb up the path for 100 metres then drop down right to the entrance to the chasm. Continue up the same path to the higher falls. For Stickle Ghyll, take the well-constructed path behind the hotel that follows the right bank of the beck, east of Dungeon Ghyll.

54   WHORNEYSIDE FORCE

Great Langdale, Lake District

Maps: OS Landranger 89 and 90, OS Explorer OL Map 6.

Grid Ref: NY 262054.

Nearest towns: Ambleside 7 miles (11km), Coniston 9 miles (14km).

Walk: Grade – Moderate. Time – 1 hour each way.

Orientation: East.

The Falls: Buscoe Sike flows down from Three Tarns south of Bow Fell (sometimes spelt Bowfell) at the head of Great Langdale. Whorneyside Force is a pretty and secluded waterfall just below Hell Gill. The beck drops more than 12 metres into a deep circular pool held back by a natural dam of boulders. The site provides shelter from the wind even when it is blowing up Great Langdale from the east. A few small rowans cling to the cliff face. There are fine views down Great Langdale. The picture was taken after the Lake District had had no rain for two weeks!

Access: From the National Trust car park at the Old Dungeon Ghyll Hotel towards the head of Great Langdale cross over the bridge and take the tarmac road to Stool End Farm. Go through the farm and follow the footpath signed to The Band, but bear left up the valley keeping the beck to the left. Where the path forks and the left branch crosses the beck, keep on the right branch. Soon a small fall in a narrow ravine is seen to the left. Cross the beck by a footbridge and immediately turn right. Keep the beck to the right and the falls are soon reached.

55   FALLS IN TOM GILL, TARN HOWS   ☆☆☆☆

Tarn Hows, Lake District

Maps: OS Landranger 96 and 97, OS Explorer OL Map 7.

Grid Ref: NY 325999.

Nearest towns: Coniston 2 miles (4km), Ambleside 6 miles (10km).

Walk: Grade – Moderate. Time – 15 mins each way.

Orientation: West.

The Falls: These impressive falls are found beside the path that leads from the lake commonly known as Tarn Hows towards Yew Tree Tarn. They are set in mature woodland made up mainly of oak and beech. Several small falls culminate in a fall of 10 metres into a small pool from which the beck exits left. A small path leads to the base of the falls. The broken white water contrasts sharply with the dark rock and vegetation. For an idea of scale, note the person with the dog at the top of the falls.

Access: Park in the National Trust car park at the south-west end of Tarn Hows. Begin to walk clockwise round the tarn and take a footpath which follows the beck that drains Tarn Hows and signed to Glen Mary and Yew Tree Tarn. The way down is rather steep, but rough stone steps have been provided.

> **Tarn Hows:** Tarn Hows is really the name of a local hill. The tarn, which is usually called by the same name, was created from three small tarns by damming the top of Tom Gill. It has a 'chocolate box' beauty which must make it the most photographed tarn, as opposed to lake, in the Lake District. If you want to avoid crowds, do not come here on bank holidays.

56   LEVERS WATERFALL   ☆☆☆☆

Coniston Water, Lake District

Maps: OS Landranger 96 and 97, OS Explorer OL Map 6.

Grid Ref: SD 282992

Nearest towns: Walk from Coniston, Ambleside 7 miles (11km).

Walk: Grade – Moderate. Time – 50 mins each way.

Orientation: South.

The Falls: On the way up to Levers Waterfall the path passes Miners Bridge across Church Beck. Just below the bridge the beck divides round a rocky outcrop and drops 7 metres into a ravine. Other falls are seen both up and downstream. Levers Waterfall itself is a succession of falls down the fellside best viewed from a wooden footbridge across the beck. The energetic might

climb to the top of the falls and find an attractive small fall not visible from below and a leat diverting water to the left of the beck, which once supplied power to the mines.

Access: From the car park in Coniston walk along the road towards

Coppermines Youth Hostel. Miners Bridge and the first falls are reached after 20 minutes. Do not cross the bridge, but continue along the stony road past the Youth Hostel, with Coniston Old Man to the left, until the falls are reached.

Mining: Coniston Old Man is riddled with mine shafts and passages. Copper was mined here since the end of the 16th century and reached its peak in the 19th century. A building near the youth hostel used to house a huge overshot waterwheel. Spoil heaps and the entrances to adits are everywhere to be seen. They should never be entered without an expert guide.

See colour plate 3B

57   FORCE FALLS   ☆☆☆

Grisedale Forest Park, Lake District

Maps: OS Landranger 96 and 97, OS Explorer OL Map 7.

Grid Ref: SD 340912.

Nearest towns: Coniston 9 miles (14km), Ambleside 10 miles (16km).

Walk: Grade – Easy. Time – 5 mins each way.

Orientation: South-east.

The Falls: Above the falls, behind a barrier of rock like a natural dam, Force Beck looks deep and still. Two breaches in this barrier allow the water to rush through and form a series of complex, attractive falls over ledges and through numerous fissures in the rock. The woods around the falls are the southern end of Grisedale Forest Park, home to a large display of open-air sculptures. Walk up into the woods and discover a waterfall with a sculpture entitled *Bean an t-Visce* (Woman of the Water) by Alannah Robins.

Woman of the Water

Access: Park in Blind Lane forestry car park near Force Mills at a T junction of minor roads between Coniston Water and Windermere (SD 341911). Walk about 80 metres up the road towards Satterthwaite and through an iron gate on the left down to the falls. Continue up the road about 1 km and take a forestry road on the left for three minutes to see the falls with the sculpture.

Lake District bobbin mills: Force Beck was harnessed to provide power for bobbin making at Force Mills. In the 19th century, the Lake District provided most of the bobbins for the Lancashire cotton mills. At a conservative estimate, 60 mills turned out well over 30 million bobbins a year. Bobbin production ceased in 1983 when Spark Bridge Mill closed.

58   HOLME FORCE   ☆☆☆

Loweswater, Lake District

Maps: OS Landranger 89, OS Explorer OL Map 4.

Grid Ref: NY 119213.

Nearest towns: Cockermouth 7 miles (12km), Keswick 12 miles (20km).

Walk: Grade – Easy, but muddy when wet, Time – 30 mins each way.

Orientation: East turning North.

The Falls: Holme Beck drops down to Loweswater in a series of falls and cascades through mixed woodland. There is a good view from a footbridge across the beck at the base of the falls. However, it is well worth the effort to climb the steep and narrow path to the right of the falls. Near the top, the water hits a shelf of rock and is thrown upwards and forwards in an arching curve, a dramatic sight when seen at close hand. Moss and ferns cling to the branches of trees that are within range of spray.

Access: There are two car parks at the north end of Loweswater. Choose the one with a telephone box. Follow a footpath across fields which can be very wet and across two stiles. Turn left along a tarmac farm road past Hudson's Place (a farm) and along a footpath leading into Holme Wood with its fine oaks, firs and pines. Turn right at the first opportunity and the path leads to the falls.

59   SCALE FORCE   ☆☆☆☆☆

Crummock Water, Lake District

Maps: OS Landranger 89, OS Explorer OL Map 4.

Grid Ref: NY 151171.

Nearest Towns: Keswick 9 miles (14km), Cockermouth 10 miles (16km).

Walk: Grade – Strenuous. Time – 1 hour 15 mins each way.

Orientation: North-east.

The Falls: These falls contain the highest single-drop fall in the Lake District. The main vertical drop is deep in a dark ravine reminiscent of Dungeon Ghyll,

but rather more dramatic. This fall is followed by a smaller, wider fall. The two together look like an exclamation mark! The ravine is overhung and partially filled with holly and silver birch which would tend to obscure the falls when in leaf. It is best to come in winter or spring. Above the main fall is another fall of about 3 metres height.

Access: Park in a car park in Buttermere. Walk to the left of The Fish Inn and follow a path signed to Scale Force along a stony track. Cross Buttermere Dubs, the river linking Buttermere with Crummock Water, by a fine stone bridge and immediately turn right. Two paths lead to Scale Force, a higher and a lower. Both are indistinct and can be very rough and boggy. The higher is marked by a line of cairns. Even if both paths are missed, the falls can be found simply by walking on along the contour line. There are fine views of Crummock Water from the path and from the falls.

Crummock Water and Buttermere

60   MOSS FORCE   ☆☆☆☆

Buttermere, Lake District

Maps: OS Landranger 89 and 90, OS Explorer OL Map 4..

Grid Ref: NY 203174.

Nearest towns: Keswick 7 miles (11km), Cockermouth 11 miles (18km).

Walk: Grade – Easy (also seen from car park). Time – 7 mins each way.

Orientation: North-east.

The Falls: This fine open fellside waterfall in three distinct sections can be seen from the road and car park. First, the beck appears over the skyline, splits round a projection of rock and slithers down a steep cliff into a small pool. A few scattered small rowans dot the banks. A few metres lower down is a fine cascade into a larger pool with juniper on the right bank. Finally, a slightly smaller fall into a pool gracefully overhung with rowan trees leads on to a small ravine with further small falls.

Access: There is a car park virtually at the foot of the falls at Newlands Hause at the top of the pass between Buttermere village and Keswick. A good path leads up the fell and divides to go to the upper and middle cascades. To get close to the upper fall requires a steep scramble over rocks. The lowest fall is reached by crossing a steep grassy slope.

The middle cascade

61   COMBE BECK and SOUR MILK GILL FALLS   ☆☆☆

Buttermere, Lake District

Maps: OS Landranger 89 and 90, OS Explorer OL Map 4.

Grid Ref: NY 182152, NY 171160.

Nearest towns: Keswick 9 miles (14km), Cockermouth 10 miles (16km).

Walk: Grade – Easy (but not suitable for wheelchairs). Time – 25 mins each way.

Orientation: North-east.

The Falls: The falls down Sour Milk Gill (not to be confused with several other gills of the same name sometimes spelt 'Sourmilk') can be seen a long way off as a gash of white down the fell side. The beck drains a hanging valley containing Bleaberry Tarn. The alluvial fan from Sour Milk Gill together with that from Mill Beck on the opposite side of the valley has separated Crummock Water from Buttermere which at one time were joined to form a single lake. There is no access up the gill, but a path leads to Bleaberry Tarn via the top of the falls. Combe Beck drains Burtness Combe. The falls are seen clearly from the path. The beck drops over a small crag with a sentinel larch to the right.

Access: From the village of Buttermere walk to the left of Fish Inn and bear left towards the end of Buttermere and the foot of Sour Milk Gill. A good stone and gravel path through Burtness Wood and along the lake shore leads to Combe Beck Falls.

Combe Beck Falls

62   **FALLS ON WARNSCALE BECK**   ☆☆☆☆

Buttermere, Lake District

Maps: OS Landranger 89 and 90, OS Explorer OL Map 4.

Grid Ref: NY 201135 and NY 205134.

Nearest towns: Keswick 11 miles (17km), Cockermouth 12 miles (19km).

Walk: Grade – Moderate/Strenuous. Time – 1 hour 10 mins each way.

Orientation: North and West.

The Falls: There are several dramatic falls along this beck. The first is a series

of three concluding with a narrow spout. Higher upstream the beck emerges from a deep gorge with a fine fall of about 17 metres squeezed by its confining rocks as it drops into a small pool. At the entrance to the gorge, the beck falls about 23 metres down an almost sheer smooth wall of volcanic slate.

Access: Park at Gatesgarth car park on the B5289 south-east of Buttermere and below Honister Pass. Walk up past the farm and take a bridleway on the right. Pass a copse of pines on the right and, where the path goes between two large rocks, veer off to the right towards the waterfalls. Cross the beck by a wooden footbridge and continue up the valley. Leave the path where it turns sharply right to see the lowest falls. Cross the beck again above the gorge and return by the main path down the right bank.

Britain's only slate mine: *Below the lowest falls the ancient Skiddaw Series rocks are overlain by a volcanic lava flow. Honister Slate Mine on Honister Pass is the only working slate mine in England. Slate is usually quarried. This slate is fine volcanic ash, which settled in water. (See Lakeland Rocky Rambles by Brian Lynas who describes the geology of this area.)*

Ancient hawthorn

63   ROWANTREE FORCE   ☆☆☆

Ulpha Fell, Lake District

Maps: OS Landranger 96, OS Explorer OL Map 6.

Grid Ref: SD 145937.

Nearest towns: Whitehaven 20 miles (32km), Barrow-in-Furness 25 miles (40km).

Walk: Grade – Strenuous. Time – 1 hour each way.

Orientation: West.

The Falls: This is a series of falls on high moorland as Sambarth Beck drops down from Whitfell towards the estuary of the River Esk at Ravenglass. The rock is volcanic, at the western limit of the Borrowdale volcanic series. The beck plunges about seven metres into a deep craggy ravine, bouncing off

ledges of rock as it falls. On leaving the small pool at the foot of the fall it drops ten metres almost vertically. The gorge is now deeper with vertical sides to which heather clings. The beck is squeezed through a narrow gap, runs through the gorge and emerges once more onto the open fellside. There are fine views of the high fells around Wastwater, Ravenglass, Sellafield, the sea and the Isle of Man.

Access: Turn off the A595(T) 4 miles south of Muncaster Castle and take a minor road signed 'Scenic route to Broughton'. Park beside the road near Fell Lane or at the telephone box near the turn off the A595(T). The third track on the left along the minor road is Fell Lane which leads to Grange Farm. Go through the gate at the end of the straight lane. The path quickly peters out. Walk due east, cross a beck and follow its right bank. When level with the beginning of the second conifer plantation to the left, turn to the south-east towards Red Gill, a gully running down Corney Fell. The track becomes clear beyond Red Gill. Follow it eastwards until a larger beck (Sambarth Beck) is reached and walk down its left bank to the falls.

Sellafield: Whatever your views on nuclear power generation or Britain's role in the nuclear reprocessing industry a visit to Sellafield would be an eye-opener. The visitor centre gives plenty of information geared to both adults and children. Trips around the site are provided.

64   MILLERGILL BECK FALLS   ☆☆☆

Whitbeck, Lake District

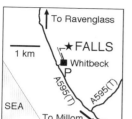

Maps: OS Landranger 96, OS Explorer OL Map 6.

Grid Ref: SD 119847.

Nearest towns: Millom 5 miles (8km), Whitehaven 27 miles (43km).

Walk: Grade – Easy, moderate to finish. Time – 15 mins each way.

Orientation: West.

The Falls: Norman Nicholson describes these falls in his book *Greater Lakeland*. He pictures the scene – "the light pings off the crags ... a scene ... as bold, as bare and as exhilaratingly open as any in Cumberland". The beck zigzags down the fellside then drops vertically before meandering northward across flat land towards the sea. Here there is a fine view westward to the Isle of Man. A patch of scree must be crossed to reach the top of the falls.

Access: Park in a lay-by next to Whitbeck Church on the A595(T) five mile north of Millom. Walk through the little hamlet of Whitbeck and just before Whitbeck Mill (now a private house) turn up a wide track onto the open fell and it is just a few metres to the falls.

Lapwing

65   FALLS ON NETHER BECK   ☆☆☆☆☆

Wastwater, Lake District

Maps: OS Landranger 89, OS Explorer OL Map 6.

Grid Ref: NY 155083 and NY 161074.

Nearest towns: Gosforth 7 miles (11km), Barrow-in-Furness 32 miles (52km).

Walk: Grade – Moderate. Time – 50 mins each way.

Orientation: South-east and South.

The Falls: The upper falls on Nether Beck are at the bottom of one of Lakeland's most spectacular gorges. The ravine is deep and narrow affording only glimpses of the falls it contains. At the lower end of the gorge, there is a fine hanging valley fall, which drops down the opposite bank to the bottom of

the gorge. A twenty minute walk downstream reveals the lower group of falls. It looks as if a huge cube of rock has been removed from the bed of the beck producing a square pool with vertical sides. The beck divides into several streams which fall into this pool from two sides. From this pool the beck plunges vertically into a large pool almost divided into two by a buttress of rock pointing upstream to the fall making the water circulate endlessly in one half of the pool. Three minutes further downstream the beck drops into a dark ravine overhung with oak and birch.

Access: Take the road along the bank of Wastwater towards Wasdalehead. About halfway along the lake park in a small parking place just before a cattle grid at Netherbeck Bridge. Walk back along the road to a bridle path sign pointing obliquely up the fell side. Follow this path, which passes near the right bank of the beck to the falls.

St Mary's Church, Gosforth: The churchyard at Gosforth contains, in addition to the most northerly cork-oak tree in Europe, a magnificent Viking cross, the tallest in England and carved about 940AD. Although it is a Christian monument with a cross at the top, the shaft is covered in carvings depicting Norse legends. It is in a remarkably good state of preservation. The church itself contains many other treasures.

66   RITSON'S FORCE   ☆☆

Wasdale, Lake District

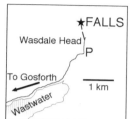

Maps: OS Landranger 89 and 90, OS Explorer OL Map 6.

Grid Ref: NY 185093.

Nearest towns: Gosforth 9 miles (14km), Whitehaven 20 miles (32km).

Walk: Grade – Moderate. Time – 10 mins each way.

Orientation: South and East.

The Falls: These falls, named after a previous landlord of the inn at Wasdale Head, are picturesque on a small scale. Three falls are set in a grassy gill among larches and mixed broad-leaved trees. The middle fall drops into a deep bowl-like pool with vertical walls from which

the beck escapes down a 4 metre fall to continue singing its way down to Wast Water. The rock here is lava belonging to the Borrowdale Volcanic Series.

Access: Park in the car park at Wasdale Head. Walk on to the inn. Behind the inn, follow the bridleway signed to Black Sail Pass, Ennerdale and Buttermere. Cross an old pack-horse bridge with an amazingly flat profile and on to the larch plantation that hides the falls.

See colour plate 4A

The pack-horse bridge

67 GABLE BECK, SPOUTHEAD GILL and GRETA GILL FALLS

Wasdale, Lake District

Maps: OS Landranger 89, OS Explorer OL Map 6.

Grid Ref: NY 201098, NY 217092 and NY 216084.

Nearest towns: Gosforth 9 miles (14km), Barrow-in-Furness 35 miles (56km).

Walk: Grade – Moderate to Gable Beck Falls then strenuous. Time – 30 mins to Gable Beck, another 1 hour to reach the other falls.

Orientation: South-west, North-west and West.

Spouthead Gill Falls

The Falls: Falls on Gable Beck are reached first. This is a series of three beautiful falls each about 8 metres high. The top fall is a narrow fan, the middle one a narrow fall constricted between rocks flanked by holly and rowan, and the lowest is a fine verti-cal drop to a stream with an open aspect. The top fall in Spouthead Gill seen against the skyline is a segmented fall over a jagged rock face. This is followed by three narrow falls in a small ravine. Greta Gill Falls drop about 150 metres zigzagging down the fellside below Broad Crag.

Access: From the car park near Wasdale Head Inn take the track past a tiny church to Burnthwaite Farm. Pass behind the farm and turn right along 'Moses Trod' Cross the footbridge over Gable Beck and climb up the left bank to the falls. Return to the path and follow it keeping close to the right bank of Lingmell Beck. Footpaths lead up Spouthead Gill toward Sty Head and up the left tributary towards Greta Gill and Scafell Pike.

Field patterns: The stone walls of the fields around Burnthwaite Farm form sinuous patterns seen from above. Large bulges on the walls contain stones cleared from the fields. In the churchyard of the Church of St Oswald are graves of mountaineers who lost their lives on the surrounding fells.

68 DALEGARTH FALLS (STANLEY FORCE) ☆☆☆

Eskdale, Lake District

Maps: OS Landranger 96, OS Explorer OL Map 6.

Grid Ref: SD 173995.

Nearest towns: Gosforth 8 miles (13km), Ambleside 14 miles (22km).

Walk: Grade – Moderate. Time – 15 mins each way.

Orientation: North.

The Falls: The falls are set in a dramatic gorge with beetling granite crags. This

is part of the Eskdale granite outcrop where a small part of the massive granite 'batholith' underlying the Lake District comes to the surface. The beck, which drains Birker Fell, drops as a narrow spout about 13 metres into a deep pool. The falls are approached through ancient oak woodland. The invasive rhododendrons, which are so out of place in open countryside, are being eradicated.

Access: Arrive by the Ravenglass and Eskdale Railway, which you take to the terminus, Dalegarth Station. If coming by car drive from Gosforth towards Hardknott Pass and Ambleside. Just before Dalegarth Station take a small road south to a car park. Follow a well-signed footpath to Stanley Ghyll. The falls

are seen a few metres beyond the third foot-bridge.

La'al Ratty: The Ravenglass and Eskdale small gauge railway (La'al Ratty) should not be missed. From Ravenglass to Dalegarth it passes through beautiful estuary and mountain scenery.

Engine on the Dalegarth turntable

69   # BIRKER FORCE   ☆☆☆☆

Eskdale, Lake District

Maps: OS Landranger 96, OS Explorer OL Map 6.

Grid Ref: SD 187999.

Nearest towns: Gosforth 8 miles (13km), Ambleside 14 miles (22km).

Walk: Grade – Moderate (Strenuous to top of falls). Time – 45 mins each way.

Orientation: North-west.

The Falls: A great vertical rent in the façade of Birker Fell can be seen from across the River Esk. Birker Force is a silver ribbon in the depths of this gully. The lower slopes are littered with granite boulders within granite cliffs. Eskdale is one of the locations in the Lake District where granite reaches the surface. The most dramatic vertical drop in this series of falls necessitates a strenuous climb to the top where the rock is volcanic. At the top of the falls it is worth walking 300 metres west along the fell for views of Eskdale from Hardknott Pass to the sea.

Access: Drive the road through Eskdale and opposite the turning to Boot take a rather rough road down to Saint Catherine's Church. Park there and leave a donation in the church. Caravans and precious cars should park at Dalegarth Station. Walk upstream to Doctor Bridge. Cross the bridge, walk up the hill passing Lower Birker Farm. Further up the fell there is a wall and larch plantation to the right and later a fine juniper wood to the left. Take the first gate through the fell wall to the right and follow the contour round to the falls.

Doctor Bridge

70   UPPER ESKDALE FALLS   ☆☆☆☆

Upper Eskdale, Lake District

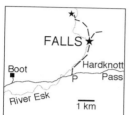

Maps: OS Landranger 89 and 90, OS Explorer OL Map 6.
Grid Ref: NY225037.
Nearest towns: Ambleside 11 miles (17km), Whitehaven 23 miles (37km).
Walk: Grade – Moderate. Time – 1 hour to Lincove Bridge.
Orientation: South.

The Falls: There is a fine collection of falls close to Lincove Bridge. On Lincove Beck, which joins the River Esk from the left, is a series of four falls. Most are tall narrow falls in clefts and gorges shaded by trees. Close to the bridge there are falls on the River Esk where it flows through a rocky cleft with wood anemones clinging to the vertical rock face. A few metres upstream are the Esk Falls. The river fans out and falls onto jagged upward-pointing slabs and pinnacles of rock. Above and below these falls are fine pools. More falls are encountered upstream in small gorges. The energetic could follow the Esk onto Great Moss, a large flat marshy area, to see Cam Spout where How Beck plunges down from Scafell to meander across Great Moss and join the Esk.

Esk Falls

Access: Park in the car park at the bottom of Hardknott Pass. Walk the farm road to Brotherilkeld Farm and follow the footpath up the dale with the River Esk to the left. For the most part the paths above Lincove Bridge are quite distinct, but Great Moss should only be crossed in good weather with a map and compass.

Eskdale Mill: Eskdale Mill at Boot is one of England's oldest working water-mills and still grinds corn. It is unusual in that two overshot waterwheels in series provide the power. The public are welcome to look around.

71   TARN BECK FALLS   ☆☆☆

Duddon Valley, Lake District

Maps: OS Landranger 96, OS Explorer OL Map 6.

Grid Ref: SD 240985.

Nearest towns: Ambleside 12 miles (19km), Barrow-in-Furness 24 miles (39km).

Walk: Grade – Moderate. Time – 30 mins each way.

Orientation: West.

The Falls: Tarn Beck drains Seathwaite Tarn and joins the River Duddon at Seathwaite. It tumbles down into the valley dividing and rejoining many times as it falls. Near the foot of the falls it divides into four streams, the largest forms a 10 metre vertical fall surrounded by juniper, alder, ash and holly. Having

become one stream again under a footbridge it divides once more round an island before joining another stream that runs down the valley. There are attractive falls at this confluence.

Access: In the Upper Duddon Valley (a favourite of Wordsworth's) park beside the road one mile north of the inn at Seathwaite. Take a narrow unsigned footpath to the south-east and bear left around the base of a rocky crag. Enter the edge of an oak wood between two upright perforated stones, which once supported a six-barred gate. Walk on with a wall and fence on your right, past a barn and a farm building (now a holiday home) down to the beck. Cross by a wooden footbridge and turn left along the left bank of the beck. Do not go over the ladder stile. At first this path is ill-defined but becomes clearer before the falls are reached.

> *One reason for going to the pub:* You may have several reasons to visit the Newfield Inn at Seathwaite. One would be to see the unusual stone floor in the bar. This is composed of large flags of striped 'slate' formed from fine volcanic ash, which settled in still water to form the attractive stone we see today.

See colour plate 4B

72   AIRA FORCE and HIGH FORCE   ☆☆☆☆☆

Ullswater, Lake District

Maps: OS Landranger 90, OS Explorer OL Map 5.

Grid Ref: NY 400205, NY 400211.

Nearest towns: Penrith 10 miles (16km), Ambleside 12 miles (19km).

Walk: Grade – Easy to Aira Force, then moderate. Time – 15 mins to main fall, further 20 mins to upper falls.

Orientation: South-west.

The Falls: These are probably the most visited falls in the Lake District. The lower, most famous fall is worthy of its reputation. Aira Beck falls vertically between high cliffs into a dark pool. The beck is divided at the top by a rock in mid-stream. When not in spate the two jets of water, thrown clear of the rock face, cross each other in an attractive scissors action. The fall is framed above by a stone arched bridge. Further upstream the beck divides into three round two islands. Two streams drop into a ravine and are joined by the third further downstream, an unusual and pleasing formation. High Force is a short distance upstream again. Here the beck is squeezed between two blocks of rock that appear almost to touch. These falls are at the junction of ancient Skiddaw Series rocks overlain by more recent volcanic rocks which are resistant to erosion.

Access: Park at the National Trust car park on the A592 on the west bank of Ullswater. A gravel path with occasional steps leads to the main falls. Slightly rougher paths follow both banks up to the higher falls. Refreshments and toilets are at the car park.

Tragedy at Aira Force: The legend of Emma and Sir Eglanore was recorded by William Wordsworth in 1828 in his poem 'The Somnambulist' ; a suitably romantic tale for such a scene beloved of the later Victorians.

73   # SCALEHOW FORCE   ☆☆☆

Ullswater, Lake District

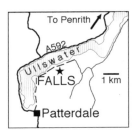

Maps: OS Landranger 90, OS Explorer OL Map 5.

Grid Ref: NY 414191.

Nearest towns: Penrith 12 miles(19km), Ambleside 23 miles (36km).

Walk: Grade – Moderate, strenuous scramble to top of falls, Time – 15 mins each way.

Orientation: North-east.

The Falls: The climb up beside these falls to the top is rewarding. Many small attractive falls of gentle charm are passed on the way up. Beside these falls are flat grassy areas shaded by trees. At the top Scalehow Beck divides into three streams that plunge down into a rocky, wooded ravine. From here there are magnificent views of Ullswater looking north to farmland beyond the Lake District and the Solway Firth.

Lip of fall with Ullswater beyond

Access: There is limited parking at Sandwick at the south end of the road which runs down the east side of Ullswater. It is best to arrive early or you may be disappointed. Follow the bridleway towards Patterdale until a footbridge crosses Scalehow Beck. An ill-defined path leads up to the falls. Alternatively, you can walk the three miles from Patterdale round the southern end of Ullswater.

Finest view in the Lake District? In Wainwright's opinion the walk from Sandwick to Patterdale affords some of the finest views in the Lake District. Who would disagree? Look across the lake with Glenridding on the farther shore and the dramatic Helvellyn range in the distance.

See colour plate 5A

74   RED TARN BECK FALLS   ☆☆

Ullswater, Lake District

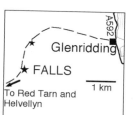

Maps: OS Landranger 90, OS Explorer OL Map 5.

Grid Ref: NY357160.

Nearest towns: Ambleside 9 miles (15km), Penrith 13 miles (21km).

Walk: Grade – Moderate, but long. Time – 1 ½ hours each way.

Orientation: North.

The Falls: The lower falls near a footbridge over Red Tarn Beck consist of a series of small falls. The largest drops vertically about 3 metres. The upper series of falls are found 1 km below Red Tarn. The beck falls in three steps over big blocks of rock covered with moss, liverworts and lichens. The aspect is open being above the tree-line.

Access: From the car park in Glenridding near the south end of Ullswater walk up Greenside Road to the spoil tips and old buildings of Greenside Mine and a Youth Hostel. Follow the footpath signs to Red Tarn and Helvellyn. Cross Helvellyn Beck and, later, Red Tarn Beck by footbridges. From the bridge across Red Tarn Beck walk up the right bank to see the lower falls. Continue up the path to where a small crag comes close to the path on the right side. At this point strike left to the upper falls. The path up from Glenridding is a popular route to Helvellyn and at some times in the year seems more like Oxford Street before Christmas. If you are not going on to climb Helvellyn it is worth just going up to Red Tarn to see this corrie lake with Helvellyn beyond, flanked by Striding Edge and Swirral Edge.

Upper Falls

Lead and Silver: At one time Greenside Mine was one of the largest lead mines in England. It also yielded some silver. An interesting display at the Information Centre in Glenridding gives details of the history of this mine and the technology employed.

75 DEEPDALE BECK FALLS ☆☆☆

Patterdale, Lake District

Patterdale
P
1 km
A592
FALLS
★
To
Kirkstone Pass

Maps: OS Landranger 90, OS Explorer OL Map 5.

Grid Ref: NY 368125.

Nearest towns: Ambleside 7 miles (12km), Penrith 15 miles (24km)

Walk: Grade – Moderate with steep climb at end. Time – 1¼ hours each way.

Orientation: East.

The Falls: At the head of Deepdale are three becks with falls. The most southerly drains a corrie named Link Cove. The central beck falls over the crags of Greenhow End (The Forces) and often carries little water. The falls described here are on the most northerly beck that drains Cawk Cove. The path follows the left bank, but they are best viewed from the right. Furthest upstream the beck drops vertically for 4 metres into a small pool then splits round a large rock, uniting below to drop another 5 metres. Juniper and heather cling to the vertical walls of the ravine. Downstream several further falls are hidden in the ravine. The beck finally emerges from the ravine down a rock slide.

Access: Park by the telephone-box at Deepdale Bridge one mile south of Patterdale on the A592. Cross the bridge and immediately take a track to Lane Head. Turn left and pass Deepdale Hall and Wall End. The track then becomes a foot-path and crosses a clap-per bridge. Continue up the dale, through mounds of glacial moraine deposits, to the falls.

Clapper Bridge on the way to the falls

76 DOVEDALE BECK FALLS ☆☆☆

Brothers Water, Lake District

Maps: OS Landranger 90, OS Explorer OL Map 5.

Grid Ref: NY 386116.

Nearest towns: Windermere 10 miles (16km), Penrith 15 miles (24km).

Walk: Grade – Moderate. Time – 45 mins each way.

Orientation: South-east.

The Falls: These falls can be seen from the A592 while driving down from Kirkstone Pass to Patterdale. The beck drops about 7 metres, turns to the right, spreads out over the rock then drops another 7 metres into a small pool. Silver birch, alder and hazel clothe the banks. Further upstream above a gate there are more falls where the beck zigzags down into a pool beneath two alders. In the distance the beck is seen cascading down from Dove Crag.

Access: Park at Cow Bridge car park on the A592 near the turn to Hartsop. Take the track south which follows the west bank of Brothers Water to Hartsop Hall farm. Note the round arched windows and the stone ram's heads above the door. The track continues into Dovedale, crosses the beck by a wooden footbridge and follows the right bank to the falls. Across one of the small streams above the falls is a tiny clapper bridge. Why is it there?

Note the figure above the falls, giving scale

Fungus growing on a tree-trunk

77   HAYESWATER GILL FALLS   ☆☆☆

Hayeswater, Lake District

Maps: OS Landranger 90, OS Explorer OL Map 5.

Grid Ref: NY 424129.

Nearest towns: Windermere 10 miles (16km), Penrith 15 miles (24km).

Walk: Grade – Moderate. Time – 35 mins each way.

Orientation: North-west.

The Falls: These falls cannot be seen from the path. About 300 metres upstream of the filter house a careful walk down the steep grassy slope reveals the falls hidden at the entrance to a deep ravine. As the water falls it is constricted by cliffs on either side, hits a shelf of hard rock, sprays out and drops again into a small pool before hurrying on down the ravine. Further upstream are other attractive falls and downstream is a long waterslide.

Access: There is a car park at the east end of the small village of Hartsop, about 4km south of Patterdale off the A592. Take a tarmac path signed to Hayeswater and just after a cattle grid fork right to a bridge across the beck and follow the stony track up Hayeswater Gill. There are views up the empty valley of Pasture Bottom and back to Helvellyn. A five minute walk beyond the falls brings you to Hayeswater Reservoir surrounded by high crags.

The Herdwick breed: *Herdwick sheep are predominantly found in the Lake District. These distinctive intelligent animals (intelligent as sheep go, that is) have thick coats and are able to withstand severe weather. They have a particularly well-developed 'hefting' instinct allowing them to be kept on open fells without walls or fences to prevent them wandering off their territory. This hefting is learned by the lambs from the ewes.*

Herdwick ewe

Plate 1A: Hardraw Fall, J.M.W. Turner; Fall 104

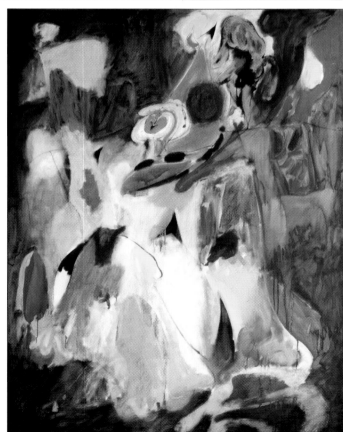

Plate 1B: Waterfall, Arshile Gorky

Plate 2A: View from Chattlehope Spout. Fall 5

Plate 2B: High Force. Fall 23

Plate 2C: Wynch Bridge at Low Force, Teesdale. Fall 24

Plate 3A: View from Fisherplace Gill. Fall 37

Plate 3B: Path to Levers Waterfall. Fall 56

Plate 4A: Wasdale, near Ritson's Force. Fall 66

Plate 4B: Duddon Valley, near Tarn Beck Falls. Fall 71

Plate 5A: Ullswater and the Helvellyn Range near Scalehow Force. Fall 73

Plate 5B: Ruskin's View, Kirkby Lonsdale, near Ease Gill Falls. Fall 89

Plate 6A: Thornton Force, Ingleton. Fall 90

Plate 6B: Hunt Pot, Ribblesdale. Fall 94

Plate 6C: The village of Linton at Linton Falls. Fall 114

Plate 7A: Tarnbrook Wyre Falls. Fall 125

Plate 7B: Golitha Falls. Fall 147

Plate 8: White Lady Falls. Fall 145

78   ## UPPER KENTMERE FALLS

Kentmere, Lake District

Maps: OS Landranger 90, OS Explorer OL Map 7.

Grid Ref: NY 441095, NY 440088, NY 447085.

Nearest towns: Windermere 8 miles (13km), Kendal 9 miles (14km).

Walk: Grade – Moderate, Time – 3 hours 30 mins round trip.

Orientation: South-west, South-east and South.

Ice formations around lower falls: River Kent.

The Falls: The infant River Kent leaves the corrie of Hall Cove below Mardale Ill Bell by a two metre fall. It then runs a few metres, drops eight metres while bouncing off rocks as it falls, runs for a short distance and falls two metres before running on down the valley. Halfway between these falls and Kentmere Reservoir is an attractive series of five falls and pools. Lingmell Beck runs independently into the reservoir and forms a series of falls in a gully with a scattering of trees. The rocks here were produced from ash thrown out by violent volcanic eruptions similar to the one that destroyed Pompeii in AD 79.

Access: There is limited parking at Kentmere where there is a tea-shop. Walk up the road past Hartrigg Farm and quarry spoil heaps to Kentmere Reservoir. Keep the reservoir on you right and follow the right bank of the river to the furthest falls. Walk down the left bank to the lower falls, then across to Lingmell Beck. Return by the same path.

79   DOCKERNOOK GILL FALLS   ☆☆

Longsleddale, Lake District

Maps: OS Landranger 90, OS Explorer OL Map 7.

Grid Ref: NY 503011.

Nearest towns: Kendal 7 miles (11km), M6 Junction39 (Shap) 13 miles (21km).

Walk: Grade – Easy, just possible for wheelchairs. Time – 30 mins each way.

Orientation: East.

More ice than water

The Falls: This is a pretty series of falls with rocky cliffs, grassy promontories and shady pools as the beck drops down a wooded gully. In the central part of the series the beck drops about 10 metres in five stages into a pool about 6 metres across. There is another fall upstream and three or so downstream. Access is easy all along this stretch of the beck and grassy levels are ideal for picnics. Note that the waterfall marked on the OS Explorer OL Map 7 is further upstream still and is not as attractive as these falls.

Access: Park by the parish church and old school in Longsleddale, Grid Ref: NY 501029. Cross the River Sprint and follow a bridlepath downstream to Docker Nook Farm or walk down the road to the same point. Once through the farmyard bear left along a grass track to the falls.

80 WATERFALLS IN UPPER LONGSLEDDALE ☆☆☆☆

Longsleddale, Lake District

Maps: OS Landranger 90, OS Explorer OL Map 7.

Grid Ref: NY 477078, NY 477083.

Nearest towns: Kendal 9 miles (15km), M6 J38 (Shap) 16 miles (25km).

Walk: Grade – Moderate. Time – 45 mins each way.

Orientation: South and South-east.

The Falls: There are splendid falls along the young River Sprint. First is a deep narrow gorge in which the River Sprint can be heard but not seen. Above this are two falls, one with a precariously balanced boulder, if it's still there! Further upstream in Cleft Gill is a fine 7m plunge fall which drops vertically, hits a rock ledge and is deflected left into a large pool. Wren Gill Beck joins the River Sprint from the right after dropping 10m over twin falls which must be viewed from the right bank. A single rowan juts out horizontally over the fall. On the way back look for a fine hanging valley fall high up above a small conifer plantation. This drains Galeforth Gill, hidden over the skyline.

Access: Four miles north of Kendal turn off the A6 onto a minor road leading up Longsleddale. Park at Sadgill where the tarmac road ends. Parking is limited. Walk on up the stony track. Cleft Gill on the left is reached by climbing over one of several iron gates. Continue up the left bank of the River Sprint and cross to the right below or above the confluence with Wren Gill Beck.

Ice-floes: A perfectly circular ice-floe half a metre in diameter had formed in a side pool in the river. Similar circular 'floes' are occasionally made of sticks and leaves due to the circular movement of water in the pools.

81   MEASAND BECK FALLS   ☆☆☆☆

Haweswater, Lake District

Maps: OS Landranger 90, OS Explorer OL Map 5.

Grid Ref: NY 462155, NY 471158, NY 485155.

Nearest towns: M6 J39 (Shap) 8 miles (13km), Penrith 12 miles (19km).

Walk: Grade – Moderate. Time – 1½ hours each way.

Orientation: North-east and East.

Fordingdale Force

The Falls: The first falls reached are The Forces. These are segmented falls around huge blocks of rock and tumbled boulders repeated almost identically a short way upstream. The next, reached in 30 minutes, is Fordingdale Force where the beck drops 8m, deflects left through a narrow cleft and falls a further 3m into a deep pool. There are other attractive falls before the beck flows into the marshy expanse of Fordingdale Bottom. Further upstream again are more falls which are worth seeing. I went in January when the ice formations were spectacular.

Access: Park in Burnbanks 1½ miles south of Bampton. Follow signs marked 'Public Footpath – Fellside track via north-west shore of Haweswater to Upper Mardale'. This wide stony track leads to The Forces in 35 minutes. Take the path up the right bank of Measand Beck to a wooden footbridge, cross it and continue around Fordingdale Bottom to Fordingdale Force. Follow the left bank to the falls furthest upstream.

82   DUDDERWICK FORCE
and BLEA WATER BECK FALLS

☆☆☆

Haweswater, Lake District.

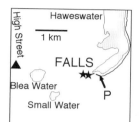

Maps: OS Landranger 90, OS Explorer OL 5.

Grid Ref: NY 463106.

Nearest towns: M6 Junction 39 13 miles (21km), Penrith 15 miles (24km).

Walk: Grade – Moderate. Time – 20 mins each way

Orientation: North and East.

The Falls: A 10-minute walk brings you to Dudderwick Force on Mardale Beck which drops in two steps over a jagged cliff. A fine birch tree juts out from the right bank. Behind the falls towers the mass of Harter Fell. A further ten minute walk leads to a short, deep, vertical-sided ravine through which flows Blea Water Beck forming a fine 7 metre fall at its head (illustrated). It may be possible to walk along the floor of the ravine to the base of the falls, but not advisable when the rocks are covered with a sheet of ice!

Access: Park in the car park at the southern end of Haweswater. Take the footpath up the valley and at a 3-way signpost follow the path towards Bampton. Cross Mardale Beck and turn left along a wide path. The falls are seen to your left. Continue up the path. The ravine with the falls on Blea Water Beck is marked by a line of trees to the left.

Blea Water Beck Falls in winter

A drowned village: Haweswater is now a reservoir, like Thirlmere, supplying water to Manchester. Before the valley was flooded in the 1930s there was a lake here nearly divided into two by the alluvial fan from Measand Beck. The village of Mardale with its church and inn, The Dunn Bull, was at the head of the lake. It sank beneath the waters of the reservoir, but not before a last poignant service had been held in the church. Many could not get in and stood on the grass in the church-yard. Stones from the church were used later to construct the round tower near the east shore housing the exit from the reservoir.

83   FORCES FALLS and   ☆☆☆☆☆
HOBGRUMBLE FALLS

Swindale, Lake District

Maps: OS Landranger 90, OS Explorer OL Map 5.

Grid Ref: NY 509114, NY 501113.

Nearest towns: M6 J39 7 miles (11km), Penrith 12 miles (19km).

Walk: Grade – Moderate, Time – 1 hour each way.

Orientation: North-west and North-east.

The Falls: These are among the finest falls in the Lake District and relatively few people ever see them. Mosedale Beck drops 100 metres in a series of ten fine falls from Mosedale down into Swindale. The whole effect is magnificent. Climb up the left bank of the falls to see them all. They are all different: some treeless, others shaded.; some narrow, others wide; some hidden in ravines; some vertical and yet others are rock-slides. Of the trees, rowan and birch predominate and juniper is abundant at higher levels. Hobgrumble Falls are seen at the south-westerly side of the head of Swindale where another beck drops 100 metres or so down a tree-lined cleft between Geordie Greathead Crag and Nabs Crag. The upper part of these falls drops vertically.

Access: From Penrith or Shap drive towards Haweswater. Between Bampton and Rosgill turn south along a narrow road that leads to Swindale. Park at the entrance to Swindale beneath fine crags. Walk the road up Swindale. At Swindale Head Farm it becomes a track. The valley opens out as a wide corrie formed by glacial action. Hobgrumble Falls lie ahead and Forces Falls to the left.

> *Old corpse road:* The track is joined at Swindale Head Farm by the Old Corpse Road, for carrying the dead from Mardale to consecrated ground at Shap for burial. At some bridges there are still stone platforms for placing the coffin while the carriers had a well-earned rest.

Yorkshire Dales and Howgill Fells

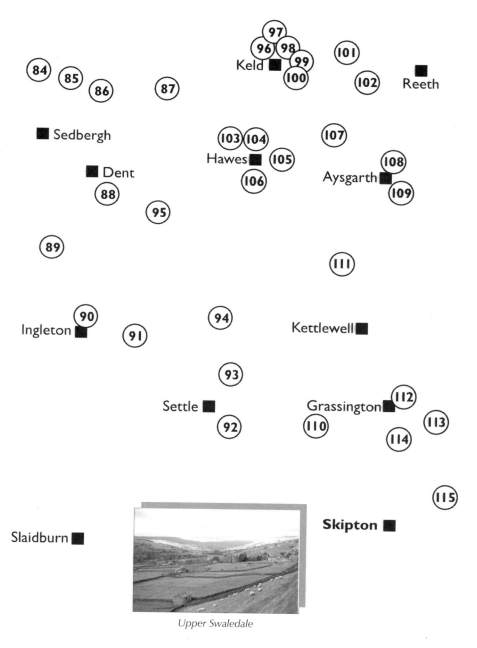

97

96 98

Keld ■ 99

100

101

102 Reeth

84

85

86

87

Sedbergh ■

103 104

Hawes ■ 105

107

Dent ■

106

Aysgarth ■ 108

88

109

95

89

111

90

Ingleton ■

94

91

Kettlewell ■

93

Settle ■

Grassington ■ 112

92

110

113

114

115

Slaidburn ■

Skipton ■

Upper Swaledale

84 THE SPOUT AND BLACK FORCE ☆☆☆☆

West side, Howgill Fells

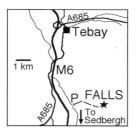

Maps: OS Landranger 97, OS Explorer OL Map 19.

Grid Ref: SD 645995 and SD 643991.

Nearest towns: Sedbergh 5 miles (9km), Kendall 11 miles (17km).

Walk: Grade – Strenuous, Time – 1½ hours each way.

Orientation: South and North-west.

The Falls: Although not far from the M6 motorway these two fine moorland falls seem utterly remote. They are found at the head of Carlingill, a deep valley cut into the western aspect of the Howgills. Carlingill Beck is formed by the confluence of Great Ulgill Beck and Little Ulgill Beck. The Spout is an eight

metre fall where Great Ulgill Beck slides and splashes obliquely down into the gill, gives a couple of twists and disappears into a ravine. A short way downstream a narrow gill joins from the south (left) side. At the head of this gill is Black Force, a series of falls and slides as Little Ulgill Beck runs down off the fells. There are fine views westward down Carlingill towards the far eastern fells of the Lake District.

Access: Two miles south of Junction 38 on the M6 (Tebay) on the A685 to Kendall take a minor road, which crosses under the motorway to Low Borrowbridge. About one and a half miles further along this road park beside the road near Carlingill Bridge. A footpath leads up the left bank of Carlingill Beck, sometimes climbing along the fellside and sometimes running level with the water. In places the path is indistinct. Further up the gill an alternative path follows the right bank.

The Spout

112

85 CAUTLEY SPOUT ☆☆☆☆☆

East side, Howgill Fells

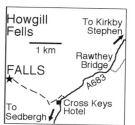

Maps: OS Landranger 98, OS Explorer OL Map 19.

Grid Ref: SD 681975.

Nearest Towns: Sedbergh 4 miles (6km), Kirkby Stephen 9 miles (15km).

Walk: Grade – Moderate (steep), Time – 1 hour each way.

Orientation: North-east and East.

The Falls: These are the highest falls in England, a series of cascades that fall for 650 feet. Their setting is truly dramatic. Cautley Home Beck plunges into a large corrie scooped out of the Howgill Fells by glacial action. On one side towers the bulk of Yarlside and opposite are the awesome Cautley Crags. The upper part of these falls has an open aspect on the high fellside, while the lower section is partly hidden in a wooded ravine. Different parts of the falls come into view the higher one climbs. Below the falls the beck continues on a gentler course to join the River Rawthey.

Access: Park close to the Cross Keys Hotel on the A683 between Sedbergh and Kirkby Stephen. A well-signed footpath takes you to a wooden bridge across the River Rawthey. Having crossed the river turn left, then right, and follow the path up to the falls. There are well-made stone steps in the higher steeper section.

The Howgills: The Howgill Fells are composed of Silurian slates and sandstones 100 million years older then the limestone of the nearby Yorkshire Dales. Paths continue over the gently rounded shapes of the fells. Their smooth outlines reminded Wainwright of sleeping elephants.

The upper falls

86   ULDALE FORCE   ☆☆☆☆

Baugh Fell, Yorkshire Dales

Maps: OS Landranger 98, OS Explorer OL Map 19.

Grid Ref: SD 736957.

Nearest towns: Sedbergh 7 miles (11km), Kirkby Stephen 8 miles (13km).

Walk: Grade – Strenuous. Time – 45 mins each way.

Orientation: North.

The Falls: A series of falls is seen along this section of the River Rawthey. At the footbridge across the river are five pretty falls in deciduous woods. Further upstream there are fewer trees. At the foot of another wooded stretch is an eight metre fall. The principal falls, though, are within this wooded section

and a climb down is required to see them. The effort is rewarded by a fine amphitheatre with a waterfall of about 15 metres. The beck falls over a horizontal bed of sandstone and for the most part drops vertically. But when arrested by ledges of hard rock, the complexity and interest of the falls is enhanced. Even though it is north facing, the width of the amphitheatre allows light into the scene. The large plunge pool is surrounded by ash and rowan and just downstream there are larches on the right bank. Further upstream again are attractive falls over huge slabs of rock in open moorland.

Access: About half way between Sedbergh and Kirkby Stephen turn onto a minor road which runs parallel and to the east of the A683. Take a turning signed to Uldale and park near a cattle grid at the end of this road. Parking is limited. Walk down through the right-hand gate to Needle House Farm, straight on (farm on right) over a footbridge and up through a small wood. Turn right down a track (with large beech trees to the right) to the bridge and the lower falls. A rough track up the left bank leads to the upper falls.

87   HELLGILL FORCE   ☆☆☆

Mallerstang Dale, Yorkshire Dales (Cumbria)

Maps: OS Landranger 98, OS Explorer OL Map 19.

Grid Ref: SD 778966.

Nearest towns: Hawes 8 miles (13km), Kirkby Stephen 7 miles (11 km).

Walk: Grade – Easy (not suitable for wheelchairs). Time – 8 mins each way.

Orientation: South-west.

The Falls: These falls mark the virtual source of the River Eden. They are reduced to a trickle in drought conditions, but are magnificent after heavy rain. The beck drops over a 13 metre high semicircular cliff capped with limestone with shale below. To the right of the falls is a row of beech and ash trees while the gorge below the falls gives shelter for rowan and larch. Rose bay willow herb and other wild flowers grow in profusion. The Settle to Carlisle Railway passes close by. In the distance is the unmistakable outline of Wild Boar Fell.

Access: Take the B6259 road that runs from Kirkby Stephen in the north to the Moorcock Inn on the A 684 at Garsdale Head in the south. Park beside the road at the border between Cumbria and North Yorkshire. Follow the track which crosses over the Settle to Carlisle Railway and immediately strike left off the track to the top of the falls.

The Settle to Carlisle Railway and Wild Boar Fell

88   LOCKINGARTH FALLS    ☆☆☆☆☆

Dentdale, Yorkshire Dales

Maps: OS Landranger 98, OS Explorer OL Map 2.

Grid Ref: SD 722837.

Nearest towns: Dent 2.5 miles (4km), Ingleton 8 miles (13km).

Walk: Park at the falls. No walk.

Orientation: North-east.

The Falls: These are my all-time favourite English falls. Why? They have a perfect form falling as a single stream then dividing equally round a rock pillar. The pool is large and round and remarkably deep, possibly as deep as the falls are high. The whole rock face is deeply undercut just above the level of the pool giving a strong horizontal line to balance the vertical of the falling water. It is possible, with care, to crouch behind the falls. There are numerous pot holes where the rock has been worn away by the grinding action of pebbles in circular eddies. They are unostentatious falls and come as a surprise, quite unannounced. They can be seen close-to by any disabled person, even from inside a car. A grass bank can be climbed beside the falls to glimpse another fall further upstream. The beck leaves its pool to pass under the road by a series of three more falls.

Access: Two and a half miles from Dent along the minor road to Ingleton where the road crosses Garstack Beck the falls are seen to the right of the road. There is off road parking for two or three cars.

Adam Sedgewick: Dent is the birthplace of Adam Sedgewick (1785 – 1873). His name is pre-eminent among English geologists of the time. It was he who coined the term Cambrian for the age when the oldest rocks in North Wales were formed. He, together with the Scottish geologist Roderick Murchison, laid the foundation for the understanding of the stratigraphy of the British Isles. Among many of his observations was the discovery of the Dent Fault. A geological trail (the Sedgewick Trail) can be followed from a car park on the A684 in Garsdale between Sedbergh and Hawes. This leads the walker along the banks of Clough River to observe the Dent Fault between Silurian slates to the west and Carboniferous limestone to the east. Obtain a trail leaflet from any Yorkshire Dales National Park Centre.

89   EASE GILL FALLS   ☆☆☆☆

Ingleborough, Yorkshire Dales

Maps: OS Landranger 97 and 98, OS Explorer OL Map 2.

Grid Ref: SD 662802 and SD 653789.

Nearest towns: Kirkby Lonsdale 5 miles (8km), Sedbergh 10 miles (16km).

Walk: Grade – Strenuous. Time – 2 hours 20 mins each way.

Orientation: South and West.

Dry waterfall

The Falls: Four contrasting falls are found in Ease Gill. The head of the gill is blocked by a cliff cut by a dramatic curved cleft with a waterfall (often only a trickle) falling into a pool that drains underground. The stream bed above this fall has been sculptured into fantastic shapes. Next encountered is a fall which is usually totally dry, but dramatic nonetheless. A walk downstream for one hour reveals two falls, the first a small fall into a long pool shaded by trees. Just downstream the beck is squeezed between rock buttresses and drops 5 metres again into a long pool.

Access: Turn off the A683 three miles north of Kirkby Lonsdale and take the small road through Barbon towards Dent. Park at Blindbeck Bridge where the road turns sharp left then right. Walk up the left bank of the beck the road has just crossed. There are attractive falls on this beck. Continue to Bull Pot Farm and walk south past a series of pot-holes and shake-holes. At Hellot Scales Barn follow a small footpath to the left down to the dry waterfall. Walk up the dry stream bed to the top fall noting the brachiopod fossils on the way. Retrace steps to the dry fall and follow the path downstream high above the left bank. Indistinct paths, run down bracken-covered ridges to the other two falls.

*Pot-holer's paradise: The Ease Gill system of caves and passages is the longest in England at over 52km. When the surface stream bed is dry the underground stream can still be heard beneath your feet. **Ruskin's View:** John Ruskin enjoyed the view of the River Lune at Kirkby Lonsdale. Before the days of political correctness he called this the finest view in England and, therefore, the world.*

See colour plate 5B

90   INGLETON WATERFALLS   

Ingleborough, Yorkshire Dales

Maps: OS Landranger 98, OS Explorer OL Map 2.

Grid Ref: SD 694753 for Thornton Force.

Nearest towns: At Ingleton. Settle 11 miles (18km).

Walk: Grade – Moderate. Time – 3hrs round trip.

Orientation: South and South-west.

The Falls: These falls are a feast. They are described in the order they are seen when walking clockwise from Ingleton up the River Twiss and down the River Doe. **Pecca Falls:** A series of five falls in a wooded valley dropping about 30 metres. Each has a deep plunge pool reputed to be as deep as the fall that made it. **Thornton Force:** In more open country the River Twiss drops vertically 14 metres over a limestone ledge into a huge pool. The curtain of water is thrown clear of the cliff face where it is under-cut and it is possible to climb behind the falls without getting too wet. **Beasley Falls:** The valley of the River Doe is very different from that of the River Twiss. For much of the length of the valley the river is forced through narrow gorges with vertical walls and drops over numerous waterfalls. Beasley Falls mark the transition from an open valley to tree-lined gorges. The river cascades over blocks of rock into a long deep pool, the right bank overhung with trees, mainly oak. Below the falls the river describes a double hairpin with further falls. **Rival Falls:** The upper of two falls within a chasm in an oak-wood drops into a large circular pool. The lower fall marks the exit from the pool and the river immediately turns sharp left. **Baxenghyll Gorge:** A footbridge over this dramatic gorge gives views of waterfalls up and down stream. **Snow Falls:** These falls are seen through the trees. The water cascades down a near-vertical 10 metre drop, the white water aptly described by the name of the falls.

Access: Come to Ingleton by public transport or park in the 'Waterfall Walk' car park beside the disused railway viaduct in Ingleton. The path is either gravel or stony and well-marked all the way. Refreshments are available near the head of the valley of the River Twiss. Some may wish to shorten the walk by returning the same way from Thornton Force, which is the most spectacular fall on the whole walk.

See colour plate 6A

91   GAPING GILL and CLAPHAM BECK FALLS   ☆☆☆

Ingleborough, Yorkshire Dales

Maps: OS Landranger 98, OS Explorer OL Map 2.

Grid Ref: SD 751727 and SD 745694.

Nearest towns: Ingleton 4 miles (7km), Settle 6 miles (10km).

Walk: No walk to Clapham Beck. To Gaping Gill - Grade – Moderate. Time – 2 hours each way.

Orientation: West and South.

Clapham Beck Falls

The Falls: Gaping Gill is one of England's most famous holes in the ground. Down it falls a beck with a sheer drop of 111 metres, twice the height of Niagara Falls. This cannot be appreciated from the surface, but the hole is impressive enough. Twice a year the public can be winched down to the huge cavern at the bottom, but at those times the stream is temporarily diverted. The stream resurfaces through Clapham Beck Cave adjacent to Ingleborough Cave beside the path leading to Gaping Gill. Clapham Beck Falls emerge from the woods just below the church in the village of Clapham and can be seen from the road.

Access: From the village of Clapham off the A65(T) between Ingleton and Settle a well-signed path leads through woods, then past Ingleborough Cave and through the impressive dry gorge of Trow Gill and on to open moorland and Gaping Gill.

Down Gaping Gill: *Two pothole clubs arrange to take members of the public down Gaping Gill by winch twice a year: Bradford Pothole Club in May and Craven Pothole Club in August to coincide with the Spring and Summer bank holidays. Obtain details from a local Tourist Information Centre.*

Lynne Dunnett being winched down Gaping Gill

119

92   SCALEBER FORCE   ☆☆☆☆

Ribblesdale, Yorkshire Dales

Maps: OS Landranger 98, OS Explorer OL Map 2.

Grid Ref: SD 840625.

Nearest towns: Settle 2 miles (3km), Ingleton 13 miles (20km).

Walk: Grade – Moderate. Time – 2 mins each way.

Orientation: West turning South.

The Falls: These are unusual and attractive falls in that they turn smoothly to the left giving almost a corkscrew effect. The broad stream tumbles over numerous small ledges down to a vertical drop followed by a series of small falls turning all the while. Some of the falls are undercut to a considerable

extent. The wooded valley into which the falls descend consists mainly of beech and birch.

Access: Two miles from Settle along the minor road to Kirkby Mallam there is room for two cars to park at the bridge across Scaleber Beck. Alternatively walk the two miles from Settle (partly along footpaths) to the same point. The top of the falls can be seen from the bridge. A signed footpath over a stile leads by a steep flight of steps to the base of the falls.

Settle Pudding: There is nothing like a hot Settle Pudding to fill you after a day on the fells in winter. Try one at the Golden Lion Inn in Settle. It's not a dessert.

93 CATRIGG FORCE and STAINFORTH FORCE

Ribblesdale, Yorkshire Dales

Maps: OS Landranger 98, OS Explorer OL Map 2 and 41.

Grid Ref: SD 832671.

Nearest towns: Settle 3 miles (5km), Ingleton 13 miles (20km).

Walk: Grade – Moderate. Time – 30 mins each way.

Orientation: West.

The Falls: Catrigg Force shows a whole variety of forms and moods in the space of a few metres. From the base of the main fall the head of the falls can be seen through the overhanging trees. The beck squeezes through a gap less than a metre wide and drops into a large plunge-pool. It widens out into a broad apron of water tumbling over rocks. It turns to the right and falls vertically into a gorge to the viewer's left. This last fall can be seen by taking a rather slippery zig-zag path through a wood of beech and sycamore. There are further small falls down the valley. The top of the main falls can be reached easily. While in the area visit Stainforth Force where the wide River Ribble drops over horizontal steps framed by an attractive stone bridge.

Access: From the public car park in Stainforth walk into the village, turn right at a T junction, over the beck, left and left again past the village green and follow the road round to the right. This becomes a track leading uphill. On reaching a gate across the track turn left over a ladder stile and the path leads down to the falls. To reach Stainforth Force from the car park, cross and walk up the B6479 and take the first left turn. Follow the road over the stone arched bridge and walk through the meadow on the left to the falls.

94   RIBBLESDALE POTS   ☆☆☆☆

Pen-y-Ghent, Yorkshire Dales

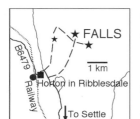

Maps: OS Landranger 98, OS Explorer OL Map 2.

Grid Ref: SD 826740, SD 824746.

Nearest towns: Settle 6 miles (10km), Ingleton 12 miles (19km).

Walk: Grade – Moderate. Time – 2 hrs 15 mins round trip.

Orientation: West and South.

The Falls: Several awesome pot-holes in Ribblesdale have waterfalls plunging down into their, often hidden, depths. **Hunt Pot:** The beck drops seven metres or so over eight limestone steps, flows across a flat table of rock then disappears vertically down the cleft-like pot deeper than the eye can see. On

Hull Pot

either side of the flat platform are huge limestone blocks scattered at random. **Hull Pot:** This is a vast hole in the ground 80 metres long and 20 metres deep. After heavy rain Hull Pot Beck falls the full 20 metres over the mid-point of the north wall. At other times it emerges in the north-east corner of the pot, but is still an impressive fall. **Sell Gill Holes:** Adjacent to the path Sell Gill Beck forms a small fall then drops underground beneath large limestone slabs that resemble a Neolithic monument. The potholers' entrance is on the other side of the path.

Access: Only go to see these falls in fine weather with good visibility. The pots have no protective fencing or any other warning of their dangers. From the car park in Horton-in-Ribblesdale walk towards Settle and soon take the Pennine Way up towards Pen-y-ghent. An attractive fall dropping from a spring can be seen to the right. At a gate, where paths cross, turn right. Before reaching a second wall turn right to see Hunt Pot. Retrace steps to the path junction and turn right up the valley. Hull Pot is soon found to the left of the path. Retrace steps again to the junction and follow the path uphill with a wall to the left. The path soon veers away from the wall and picks up another wall on the left. At the wall corner, turn left and the path leads through a gate where two walls join at right angles. Keep straight on across wet moorland to a gap in a wall. Turn left keeping the wall to the left until the Pennine Way is reached. Turn left again and follow the Pennine Way to Sell Gill Pot and down to Horton-in-Ribblesdale.

See colour plate 6B

95   FORCE GILL FALLS   ☆☆☆☆

Upper Ribblesdale, Yorkshire Dales

Maps: OS Landranger 98, OS Explorer OL Map 2.

Grid Ref: SD 757820 and SD 753823.

Nearest towns: Ingleton 6 miles (10km), Hawes 10 miles (16km).

Walk: Grade – Moderate. Time – 1 hour 15 mins each way.

Orientation: South-east and South.

Lower Falls, note figure for scale

The Falls: The first fall is seen to advantage from the path from Ribblehead to Whernside and Dent. The wide beck slips over a lip of a thick bed of sandstone to drop, partly freely and partly arrested by rock ledges, for about 16 metres into a small pool. Another viewpoint is from above where heather is abundant. The falls are framed by a wide amphitheatre of cliffs made up of bands of sandstone and shale. Further upstream are several small falls until, after 20 minutes walk, the upper falls are reached. These are similar to the lower falls, but with less verticality, the lower part being a steep rock slide.

Access: From Ribblehead railway station or car park on the B6255 Ingleton to Hawes road at the junction with the B6479 to Settle take the track towards the base of Ribblehead viaduct. Continue keeping the railway to the left. Cross the railway by a bridge alongside an aqueduct, which carries Force Gill Beck across the railway track. The first fall, which soon comes into view, is approached by a small path to the left just before a gate. Return to the main path and continue high above the left bank of the beck to the higher fall.

Settle to Carlisle Railway: *The Settle to Carlisle railway is famed for its mountain scenery and impressive viaducts. The 72-mile-long railway was*

completed in 1876 with 17 viaducts and 11 stations. Ribblehead viaduct, with 24 arches, is a quarter of a mile long, the longest on the line. Dent station is the highest on an English main line at 1150 feet (351 metres) above sea level.

Arten Gill Viaduct in Dentdale.

WAIN WATH FORCE ☆☆

96

Swaledale, Yorkshire Dales

Maps: OS Landranger 91, OS Explorer OL Map 30.

Grid Ref: NY 884015.

Nearest towns: Kirkby Stephen 9 miles (15km), Reeth 13 miles (21km).

Walk: Grade – Easy, and visible from road, Time – park at the falls.

Orientation: South.

The Falls: The name Wain Wath means Wagon Ford and here the River Swale is wide and shallow. It flows over almost horizontal strata of limestone which are seen clearly in the bed of the river and in the fine cliff behind the falls. When in spate the falls stretch right across the river, but sometimes they are restricted to four separate narrow falls where the lip of the falls has eroded to a greater extent. Below the falls is a huge pool, calm, cool and ideal for swimming on a hot summer's day when the flow is low.

Access: There is room for two or three cars beside the B6270 road 1 km west of the village of Keld. Alternatively walk along the road from Keld. A gate opens onto a meadow beside the river.

Typical Yorkshire gate through a stone wall

97 CURRACK FORCE ☆☆☆

Swaledale, Yorkshire Dales

Maps: OS Landranger 91, OS Explorer OL Map 30.

Grid Ref: NY 886016.

Nearest towns: Kirkby Stephen 9 miles (15km), Reeth 13 miles (21km).

Walk: Grade – Easy (not suitable for wheelchairs). Time – 15 mins each way.

Orientation: South.

The Falls: Stonesdale Beck, before joining the River Swale, plummets 7 metres over a limestone cliff made of impressively thick beds into a large deep pool. Just in front of the centre of the falls is a high, free-standing stack of rock as if made with a giant child's building blocks. Incorporated into the face of the base of the falls is a petrified trunk of a tree. Below the falls is a deep wooded valley.

Currack Force with little flow

Access: From the village of Keld in Upper Swaledale walk along the B6270 road westward towards Kirkby Stephen. Take the first turning right signed to West Stonesdale and Tan Hill. Walk up to the second hairpin bend where a bridleway leads off to the right signed to East Stonesdale Farm. Take this path

Swaledale Ram

and just before a stone wall and wooden bridge turn right into a field. Keep the wall to your left and after a few metres the falls are reached. You could park in the lay-by at Wain Wath Force on the B6270 and walk back to the turning to West Stonesdale.

98 CATRAKE FORCE AND HOGGARTH'S LEAP ☆☆☆

Swaledale, Yorkshire Dales

Maps: OS Landranger 91, OS Explorer OL Map 30.

Grid Ref: NY 892013.

Nearest towns: Hawes 8 miles (13km), Kirkby Stephen 10 miles (16km).

Walk: Grade – Easy (not suitable for wheelchairs), Time – 8 mins each way.

Orientation: East.

Hoggarth's Leap

Catrake Force

The Falls: The hectic River Swale in the region of Keld is strung with waterfalls like pearls on a necklace. Hoggarth's Leap at the upstream end of a campground is a series of steps in the limestone strata extending across the river which is about 20 metres wide at this point. In summer the falls are viewed across an expanse of yellow balsam flowers. Downstream of the campground is Catrake Force where the river is narrow and drops into a large, still pool.

Access: At the village of Keld in Upper Swaledale is a car park with toilets and a nearby café. From the car park take the track down to the river away from the village. Take particular care when walking along the slippery, steep bank towards Catrake Force.

99 KISDON FORCE and EAST GILL FORCE ☆☆☆

Swaledale, Yorkshire Dales

Maps: OS Landranger 91 and 92, OS Explorer OL Map 30.

Grid Ref: NY 899009.

Nearest towns: Hawes 8 miles (13km), Kirkby Stephen 10 miles (16km).

Walk: Grade – Moderate, Time – 20 mins each way.

Orientation: East.

The Falls: Of the many falls within easy walking distance of the village of Keld, Kisdon Force is the most dramatic. The River Swale emerges from a narrow gorge to fall three metres into a large pool. High cliffs dominate the left bank. Thick beds of limestone form terraces over which the river falls again in three leaps into a trough with vertical sides. The River Swale is one of the fastest flowing rivers in England and has many waterfalls along its turbulent course.

East Gill Beck, just

Kisdon Force

before joining the River Swale, provides a series of three delightful falls in a wood of, mainly, silver birch adding delicacy to the scene.

Access: Park in the village of Keld off the B6270 10 miles east of Kirkby Stephen. There is a car park with toilets and a café. Take a footpath signed to Muker until another sign directs to Kisdon Upper Falls. This steep and slippery path leads to upper and lower falls. It is easier to continue along the main path and take a narrow path back to the falls. East Gill Falls, which can be seen from the path to Muker, may be visited by turning left from the footpath to Muker and crossing the River Swale by a footbridge.

100   CLIFF BECK FALLS

Swaledale, Yorkshire Dales

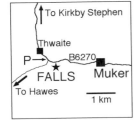

Maps: OS Landranger 98, OS Explorer OL Map 30.

Grid Ref: SD 895978.

Nearest towns: Hawes 6 miles (10km), Kirkby Stephen 12 miles (19km).

Walk: Grade – Easy (not suitable for wheelchairs). Time – 3 mins each way.

Orientation: East.

The Falls: These are dark, shady, enclosed falls. Cliff Beck plunges over a seven metre high, semicircular cliff overhung with wych elm and ash into a small pool hemmed in with large, moss-covered boulders. There is an over-

hang at the bottom of the cliff where melt-water at the end of the last ice-age washed away softer rock.

Access: Walk one mile west from Muker along the B6270 in Upper Swaledale, or park in a lay-by at Thwaite where the B6270 is joined by the road from Hawes. Go through a small gate in the wall on the south side of the road from Muker just before the junction with the road from Hawes and cross a small meadow to the falls.

Yorkshire field barns:
From your parked car you can see more than 40 stone field barns which are a typical feature of the Yorkshire Dales. They were built in hay meadows to store the hay and to provide winter shelter for cattle. Cattle are rarely wintered in these barns today, but they are still used to store hay and farm machinery.

101 BOTCHER GILL FALLS ☆☆☆☆

Swaledale, Yorkshire Dales

Maps: OS Landranger 91, 92, 98. OS Explorer OL Map 30.

Grid Ref: NY 935005.

Nearest towns: Hawes 10 miles (16km), Richmond 18 miles (29km).

Walk: Grade – Moderate. Time – 45 mins each way.

Orientation: North-east.

The Falls: Three contrasting falls drop over limestone cliffs. Just below the path the beck drops about 13 metres over a series of ledges. A few metres downstream the beck falls between high grey cliffs into a small dark pool. Here are numerous fossils: a layer of large bivalve shells in the cliff face all concave up as they floated down to the sea bed. Fallen rocks contain splendid fossil corrals. Further down is a waterfall almost hidden by massive limestone cliffs. A 20-minute walk further up Gunnerside Gill reveals falls on Gunnerside Beck.

Access: Park in Gunnerside, a village on the B6270 that runs through Swaledale. Walk west along a minor road then strike up the fellside after the last house in the village. Turn right along a good track and follow it up Gunnerside Gill till the track crosses Botcher Gill.

Upper Falls in Botcher Gill

Hushes: Gunnerside Gill once echoed to the sounds of lead mining. On either side of the gill upstream of Botcher Gill the remains of hushes can be seen. Streams were dammed high up on the fellside and the dams breached to release a torrent of water, which eroded the hillside to expose the seams of lead ore. Lumps of galena can be found along the path.

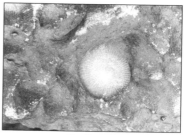

Fossil coral

102   HAVERDALE BECK FALLS   ☆☆☆

Swaledale, Yorkshire Dales

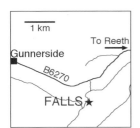

Maps: OS Landranger 98, OS Explorer OL map 30.

Grid Ref: SD 975969.

Nearest towns: Reeth 5 miles (8km), Hawes 9 miles (15km).

Walk: Grade – Easy, suitable for wheelchairs. Time – 2 mins each way.

Orientation: North-west.

The Falls: These fine woodland falls drop without interruption for about 4 metres onto a rock ledge then bounce another couple of metres into a pool. In dry weather there is still enough water to make these falls attractive. In spate

they are wider than they are high. Access is rather limited as they can only be seen from the path on the left side. The path crosses the beck by a footbridge just above the falls. The woods are mixed containing beech, silver birch, syca-more, ash and larch.

Access: The B6270 runs through Swaledale. Six kilometres west of the small town of Reeth turn onto a minor road heading south signed to Crackpot and Summer Lodge. Cross the River Swale, turn sharp right then left and up a steep hill. Park off the road on the left just before a gate leading to a footpath on the left. Alternatively continue half a kilometre to Crackpot, park there and walk back to the gate. Walk 50 metres down the gravel and stone path to the falls.

103   COTTER FORCE   ☆☆☆☆

Wensleydale, Yorkshire Dales

Maps: OS Landranger 98, OS Explorer OL Map 19 and 30.

Grid Ref: SD 848919.

Nearest towns: Hawes 2 miles (3km), Sedbergh 14 miles (22km).

Walk: Grade – Easy, suitable for wheelchairs, Time – 8 mins each way.

Orientation: South.

The Falls: These are classic wedding cake falls. Starting about four metres wide they drop over six horizontal shelves, widening as they fall to form a stream thirteen metres wide at the foot. The cliffs on either side fan out to give

the falls a pleasant, open aspect. Rowan and hazel predominate. In the Spring wild flowers abound: water avens, water forget-me-nots, wood cranesbill, red campion and many others. A path (not for wheelchairs) leads up the left side of the falls to a footbridge across Cotterdale Beck. Here the beck is squeezed through a gap only half a metre wide. There is a row of 5 or 6 round potholes along the stream.

Access: Park at the bridge across Cotterdale Beck on the A684 2 miles west of Hawes. A gate opens onto a well-constructed gravel path along the left bank of the beck to the base of the falls. Rather fine stone seats are provided along the way. A notice states that the falls have been made "accessible to all" with the permission of the owner, the work being done by paid and voluntary staff of North-west Area Management Team of the Yorkshire Dales National Park Authority with a grant from the Millennium Commission and the support of Hawes and Abbotside Parish Council. Would that this could be done at other waterfall sites!

104   HARDRAW FORCE   ☆☆☆☆☆

Wensleydale, Yorkshire Dales

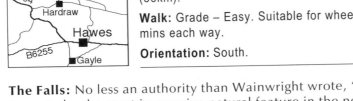

Maps: OS Landranger 98, OS Explorer OL Map 19 and 30.

Grid Ref: SD 869916

Nearest Towns: Hawes 1.5 miles (3km), Settle 23 miles (36km).

Walk: Grade – Easy. Suitable for wheelchairs. Time – 5 mins each way.

Orientation: South.

The Falls: No less an authority than Wainwright wrote, 'I consider Hardraw Force to be the most impressive natural feature in the north' *(Wainwright in the Limestone Dales.)* These justifiably famous falls are impressive by their

simplicity and scale. Fossdale Beck plunges over a towering cliff made of bands of limestone and sandstone to drop in an uninterrupted fall of 30 metres (98 feet) into a pool surrounded by boulders. It used to be 100 feet high until two feet of rock fell off the lip of the falls. This is still the highest single-drop surface waterfall in England. (There are higher falls underground.) The cliff behind the fall is undercut to a considerable extent and a simple scramble brings you behind the fall without getting wet.

Access: Enjoy the pleasant walk from Hawes or park in the village of Hardraw at the Green Dragon Inn or at Shepherd's Kitchen Café. Access to the waterfall is through the Green Dragon Inn where an entrance fee is payable at the bar.

Local attractions: Between the Green Dragon Inn and the falls is a bandstand where brass band concerts are held from time to time. Explore Hawes with its National Park Centre and Museum of life in the Dales, rope works, cheese factory and other attractions. Hardraw Force has been a popular subject for artists, JMW Turner was one.

See colour plate 1A

105   YORKSHIRE TOWNS FALLS

Wensleydale and Swaledale, Yorkshire Dales

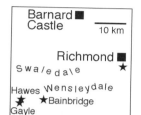

Maps: OS Landranger 92, 98. OS Explorer OL Map 30 OS Explorer 304.

Grid Refs: NZ 172006, SD 935901, SD 874898, SD 871893.

Nearest towns: At Richmond, Bainbridge, Hawes and Gayle.

Walk: No walk needed. All accessible to wheelchairs.

Orientation: All North.

The Falls: Several towns in the Yorkshire Dales are built on the banks of rivers with waterfalls. Here are four examples. At Richmond the River Swale is wide

The River Swale at Richmond

as it flows below the castle walls. It drops three metres or more over a shelf of rock, which stretches horizontally from one bank to the other. When the water level is low the flow is confined to near each bank. Yellow mimulus flowers along the dry sections of the lip of the falls. A flight of steps leads down to the water from the car park on the left bank of the river. There is a pleasant riverside walk along the wooded right bank, which affords fine views of the town and castle.

The Wensleydale towns of Hawes, Gayle and Bainbridge all have falls seen from bridges in the town centres. Gayle Beck flows through Gayle and then through Hawes. The status of River has been awarded to the Bain that flows through Bainbridge. All these towns have much to delight the visitor.

Access: What more need be said? Use local buses and explore the towns on foot.

106   AYSGILL FORCE   ☆☆☆☆

Wensleydale, Yorkshire Dales

Maps: OS Landranger 98, OS Explorer OL Map 2 and 30.

Grid Ref: SD 864884.

Nearest towns: Hawes 1 mile (2km), Settle 23 miles (37km).

Walk: Grade – Moderate (difficult scramble to base of fall), Time – 10 mins each way.

Orientation: North.

The Falls: Gayle Beck drops about 14 metres over these falls from open country into a wooded gorge. The shape of the falls is unusual and attractive. First the water flows over thick horizontal strata of limestone then fans out like a full skirt over smooth rock into a large pool. The path to the falls is flanked by water avens, ladies' mantle, wood cranesbill and Queen Anne's lace.

Access: Take the road south from Hawes towards Kettlewell and park beside the road just south of West Shaw Farm. Walk back past the farm and over a ladder stile marked "Footpath to Gayle 1 mile". Drop down into the valley, cross the beck by a footbridge and follow the path down the left bank of the beck to the falls. The climb down to the base of the falls is helped by a length of thoughtfully positioned orange baling twine. Alternatively, start from Hayle and follow the footpath up the left bank of the beck to the falls.

Water avens

107 MILL GILL FORCE and WHITFIELD GILL FORCE

Wensleydale, Yorkshire Dales

Maps: OS Landranger 98, OS Explorer OL Map 30.

Grid Ref: SD 938915, SD 934923.

Nearest towns: Hawes 5 miles (8km), Richmond and Sedbergh 20 miles (32km).

Walk: Grade – Moderate (slippery scramble to foot of Whitfield Force), Time – 50 mins each way.

Orientation: South and South-east.

Mill Gill Force

The Falls: At Mill Gill Force the water gushes through a narrow gap between high cliffs to drop about 20 metres over many rock ledges into a wooded gorge, by which time it has no force left to excavate a plunge pool. Whitfield Force is a fine single vertical drop of about 23 metres guarded above by two beech trees. Beech dominates the gorge below the falls. The water forms a diaphanous curtain that only partly obscures the dark rock behind.

Access: At the village of Askrigg take the street above the church heading west. At the end follow the footpath signed to Mill Gill Force. Pass under a mill leat (mind the drips), through several stiles, then when there is a wall to the left and a wood to the right the path forks. Bear right down to the falls. Return to this fork and take the left branch. Where it forks again take the right path signed to Whitfield Gill. Squeeze through several stiles and cross a small beck on stepping stones after which the path gets a little rougher. At another fork bear left signed 'Whitfield Force Only'. Where the path ends a steep descent to the right reaches the top of the falls. Go back along the path to some wooden steps and a steep path leading down to the beck. Follow the beck up to the falls (slippery!).

108   AYSGARTH FALLS   ☆☆☆☆☆

Wensleydale, Yorkshire Dales

Maps: OS Landranger 98, OS Explorer OL Map 30.

Grid Ref: SE 010886, SE 017887.

Nearest towns: Hawes 9 miles (15km), Northallerton 25 miles (40km).

Walk: Grade – Easy, but moderate to base of Lower Force. Difficult wheelchair access to Upper Force only. Time – 20 mins each way.

Orientation: North-east and East.

The Falls: These are reputed to be the most visited waterfalls in England. The wide River Ure drops over a sequence of horizontal limestone ledges at Upper Force, Middle Force and Lower Force. Each group of falls is different. Upper Force is set in meadows ideal for picnics. Middle Force is seen best from a viewing platform with Aysgarth Church in the background. Lower Force can be seen from river level, looking up at a multi-tiered series of falls as the river drops over numerous ledges, widening as it falls, and giving the appearance of a wedding cake. In the last ice age, the fast-moving glacier in Bishopdale scoured out a deeper valley than the slower glacier in Upper Wensleydale producing hanging valley waterfalls at Aysgarth and West Burton.

Access: Start at the car park of the Yorkshire Dales National Park Centre on the north side of the River Ure at Aysgarth on the A684. There are good facilities here with toilets and a café. well-maintained signed paths lead to all three falls.

> ***Rood screen:*** *Aysgarth parish church contains a fine rood screen removed from Jervaulx Abbey at the time of the dissolution of the monasteries by Henry VIII.*

109 CAULDRON FALLS ☆☆☆

Wensleydale, Yorkshire Dales

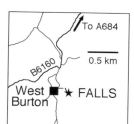

Maps: OS Landranger 98, OS Explorer OL Map 30.

Grid Ref: SE 020867.

Nearest towns: Leyburn 7 miles (12km), Grassington 18 miles (29km).

Walk: Grade – Easy with access for wheelchairs. Time – 5 mins.

Orientation: North-west.

The Falls: The village of West Burton with its solid stone houses, so typical of Yorkshire, is built round a long village green on the B6160 2km south of Aysgarth. The falls near the centre of the village are a hidden surprise. Walden Beck tumbles over a series of ledges, turns to the left, fans out and plunges into a large dark pool. To the right of the falls is an impressive overhanging slab of limestone giving shelter from the rain.

Access: From the South-east corner of the village green diagonally opposite from the Fox and Hounds take a short unmade road down to a fine pack-horse bridge and follow the beck up to the falls.

110   GORDALE SCAR FALLS and
JANET'S FOSS

Malham, Yorkshire Dales

Maps: OS Landranger 98, OS Explorer OL Map 2.

Grid Ref: SD 915641 and SD 912633.

Nearest towns: Settle 6 miles (10km), Skipton 11 miles (18km).

Walk: Grade – Moderate to Janet's Foss. Easy with wheelchair access from road to within sight of Gordale Scar. Time – 40 mins each way.

Orientation: South-west and West.

The Falls: Gordale Scar is one of the most awe inspiring natural sights in England. A cliff of Great Scar limestone was formed by the Middle Craven Fault. A great gash through the cliff was probably scoured out by glacial melt water. Through this cleft tumbles a much reduced, but still magnificent, waterfall. The vertical walls of the cleft are nearly 50 metres high, but the floor only 10 metres wide. The beck shoots through a natural aperture in the rock to fall 30 metres in several falls to the floor of the ravine. A difficult scramble can lead to the top of the falls. The painting by James Ward at the Tate Britain depicts the scene more powerfully than any photograph. Janet's Foss is a total contrast – a gentle fall over a lip of tufa (limestone, calcium carbonate, precipitated from the water onto the surface of the rock) into a large pool set in woodland.

Gordale Scar

Access: In Malham village is a car park at the Yorkshire Dales National Park Centre. Cross the road and follow the footpath beside Gordale Beck to Janet's Foss then across the road to Gordale Scar.

England's biggest dry waterfall: Malham Cove is another fine feature in this section of limestone cliff. What a waterfall must once have flowed over Malham Cove! Gordale Scar has inspired many artists including J. M. W. Turner and John Piper. Janet's Foss takes its name from Janet or Jennet, Queen of the Fairies, who is supposed to live in a cave behind the falls. Sheep used to be washed in the plunge pool.

111   CRAY FALLS   ☆☆☆☆

Wharfedale, Yorkshire Dales

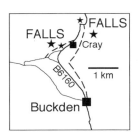

Maps: OS Landranger 98, OS Explorer OL Map 30.

Grid Ref: SD 945796, SD 934786.

Nearest towns: Grassington 11 miles (17km), Leyburn 16 miles (26km).

Walk: Grade – Moderate. Time – 2 hours round trip.

Orientation: South-west and South-east.

The Falls: Here are many falls of contrasting character. Where the road above Cray turns sharply there is a miniature Malham Cove which carries a waterfall after rain. There is a fine series of falls down the open fellside facing to the west. The hillside is terraced, typical of the Yoredale series of rocks and falls form over each resistant limestone bed. By sharp contrast the wooded, secluded Cray Gill hides many small pretty falls. Crook Gill joins Cray Gill on the right. At a small stone bridge follow the beck a few metres into Crook Gill to see an 8 metre fall into a circular plunge pool almost surrounded by vertical cliffs.

Fellside Falls above Cray

Access: The village of Buckden in upper Wharfedale has a car park with toilets (disabled included) at its northern end. Follow the clear path from here through National Trust land up

Crook Gill Falls

the dale. Do not take a short steep path down to Cray, but continue past the falls on your right to the road. Walk down the road to the White Lion Inn. Pass behind the inn along a footpath, which leads into Cray Gill and its waterfalls. Do not forget to turn up the stream by the small stone bridge to see the falls there. Continue to the road, turn left then right along the B6160 to Buckden.

112 CASEKER GILL FALLS ☆☆☆
Wharfedale, Yorkshire Dales

To Leyburn

1 km

★FALLS

B6160

■ Kettlewell

Maps: OS Landranger 98, OS Explorer OL Map 30.

Grid Ref: SD 983743.

Nearest towns: Grassington 7 miles (12km), Skipton 16 miles (25km).

Walk: Grade – Moderate, Time – 30 mins each way.

Orientation: West.

The Falls: Caseker Gill is a magical, secret place of cliffs, waterfalls, a cave, an underground stream and wild flowers in abundance. Caseker Gill Beck is joined by Park Gill Beck from the right. Just above the confluence Caseker Gill Beck gushes out of the ground at the end of its subterranean course. Above this is Dow Cave. There are veil-like falls on Park Gill Beck and more falls further upstream and downstream.

Access: Walk from the village of Kettlewell, or park about 1 mile from Kettlewell at Park Foot Bridge on the minor road to Leyburn. Continue up the road for a few metres then cross a stile with a sign 'Foot path to Park Head via East Scale Lodge'. This good path leads to another stile, the beck is below and to your right. Cross by a foot bridge, climb a natural limestone staircase and follow the path to the falls.

Birdseye Primrose, a native of Yorkshire.

113 SCALE HAW FALLS ☆☆☆

Wharfedale, Yorkshire Dales

Maps: OS Landranger 98, OS Explorer OL Map 2.

Grid Ref: SE 025639

Nearest towns: Grassington 2 miles (3 km), Pateley Bridge 9 miles (15km).

Walk: Grade – Easy (not suitable for wheelchairs) with steep scramble at end. Time – 10 mins each way.

Orientation: South.

The Falls: These are handsome falls. Hebden Beck forms a curtain of water about four metres wide dropping mainly vertically for five metres. It is a smaller version of Janet's Foss at Malham. The small gill is lightly wooded with ash, sycamore, hazel, hawthorn and dog rose. A 15-minute walk further up the valley leads to a small side stream with a waterfall. This may disappear in dry weather.

Kingfisher

Access: Take the B6265 Grassington to Pateley Bridge road and park opposite the post office in the village of Hebden. Walk up a tarmac road signed 'Bridleway to Yarnbury.' The falls are seen to the right and there is a steep scramble down to the base of the falls.

114 LINTON FALLS ☆☆

Wharfedale, Yorkshire Dales

Maps: OS Landranger 98, OS Explorer OL Map 2.

Grid Ref: SE 002635.

Nearest towns: Grassington 1 mile (2km), Skipton 9 miles (14km).

Walk: Grade – Easy, accessible for wheelchairs. Time – 5 mins.

Orientation: East.

The Falls: The River Wharfe, wide at this point, forms a series of falls over beds of limestone. The stone has been eroded into fantastic shapes. There are numerous potholes scoured out by the circular grinding of trapped pebbles. The slightly acid rain-water has dissolved the limestone and formed an arch at one point. Just upstream are two attractive weirs. The overall scene, however , is not improved by an ugly concrete wall and an unsympathetic bridge. Look, though, for a small stone footbridge with a squeeze-stile at one end. The view of Linton from up the hill is delightful (see colour plate 6C).

Access: There is a car park in Linton close to the falls, or walk along the footpath beside the river from Grassington. There is wheelchair access from the Linton car park.

11th-century church: *While in Linton visit the parish church of St Michael and All Angels, partly 11th century, but mainly dating from the 12th century.*

See colour plate 6C

115   POSFORTH GILL and   ☆☆☆☆☆
VALLEY OF DESOLATION FALLS

Wharfedale, Yorkshire Dales

Maps: OS Landranger 104, OS Explorer 297, OS Explorer OL Map 2

Grid Ref: SE 079566.

Nearest towns: Harrogate 17 miles (28km), Bradford 20 miles (32km).

Walk: Grade – Moderate. Time – 30 mins each way.

Orientation: South.

The Falls: The beck in Posforth Gill falls in two impressive columns, which join as they plunge into a pool at the base. We saw a dipper flying to and from its nest behind the fall. The path climbs steeply up the right side of the fall. Further upstream the Valley of Desolation lives up to its name. Where two becks join (Sheepshaw Beck and Dicken Dike) is another waterfall tumbling over huge boulders.

Access: At Bolton Bridge turn north off the A59 along the B6160. One mile north of Bolton Abbey park at Standholme car park by the Cavendish Pavilion. Cross the River Wharfe by the wooden bridge, follow the river upstream, and follow footpath signs to the Valley of Desolation. The path leads up to a road. Take the path to the right of Waterfall Cottage. A wooded valley is on the left and open moorland to the right. A steep path leads down to the Posforth Gill fall. Cross the beck at the fall and continue up the right bank. The main path to Simon's Seat branches left, but bear right to the upper falls in the Valley of Desolation.

Dippers: The dipper is a smart little bird that is common along stony streams and often nests behind waterfalls to be safe from predators. Typically it is seen dipping up and down on a rock. Its white waistcoat makes it conspicuous.

North York Moors

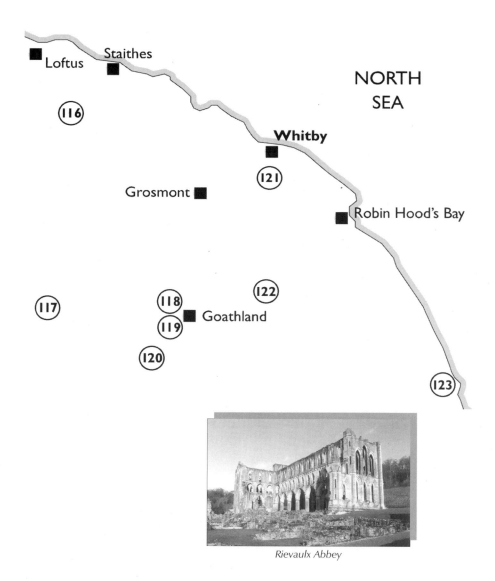

Loftus

Staithes

NORTH
SEA

(116)

Whitby

(121)

Grosmont

Robin Hood's Bay

(122)

(118)

(117)

Goathland

(119)

(120)

(123)

Rievaulx Abbey

116   SCALING BECK FALLS   ☆☆☆

North York Moors

Maps: OS Landranger 94. OS Explorer OL Map 27.

Grid Ref: NZ 749143.

Nearest towns: Loftus 6 miles (10km), Whitby 11 miles (18km).

Walk: Grade – Moderate (brambles). Time – 5 mins each way.

Orientation: North.

The Falls: These fine falls are set close to a path in woodland with dense undergrowth. The stream is thrown clear of the rock face and drops vertically for 6 metres into a small pool. Thick beds of sandstone form the upper third of the waterfall cliff. Just above the falls the beck is crossed by a footbridge and ford. The falls are seen best from the right side which involves some battling through brambles. Here there are some stone steps and fragment of wall, the site of an old mill. It is not advisable to go down to the base of the falls, the valley walls are nearly sheer. I walked on and looked for Keld Hole Waterfall marked on the OS Explorer OL Map 27, but failed to find it. The walk through these out of the way pastures and woods, though, was delightful.

Access: Turn off the A171 Whitby to Middlesborough road as it runs along the side of Scaling Dam Reservoir at Grid Reference NZ 744128. Pass through the tiny hamlet of Scaling and one kilometre further on park on the left beside the road opposite a track leading off to the right. Walk down the track to the falls.

117   GREAT FRYUP DALE FALLS

Danby, North York Moors

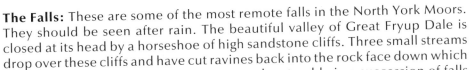

Maps: OS Landranger 94, OS Explorer OL Map 26.

Grid Ref: NZ 716018.

Nearest towns: Kirkby Moorside 13 miles (21km), Whitby 17 miles (27km).

Walk: Grade – Moderate. Time – 45 mins each way.

Orientation: North-east.

The Falls: These are some of the most remote falls in the North York Moors. They should be seen after rain. The beautiful valley of Great Fryup Dale is closed at its head by a horseshoe of high sandstone cliffs. Three small streams drop over these cliffs and have cut ravines back into the rock face down which

they tumble in a succession of falls and slides.

Access: Park off the road at the junction of two minor roads high on the moors at grid ref: NZ 697013 beside a large standing stone. This is a Millennium Cross erected in 2000. Walk north along the road for less than 1 km and turn right along a track called Cut Road. Near here look for the remains of Botton Cross of medieval origin. Pass Trough House hunting lodge. Above the head of Great Fryup Dale a bridleway crosses Cut Road. Turn left along this indistinct bridleway which zigzags down into Great Fryup Dale. Near the bottom look back to see the most westerly of the falls. Take a narrow contour path to the other two falls.

Ancient crosses: The North York Moors are dotted with no fewer than 37 old crosses. Many are at the junction of ancient tracks across the moors and acted as waymarks for travellers. Traditionally if you find coins on top of a cross you take them and if you find none then you leave some for another traveller. (See An Illustrated Guide to the Crosses on the North Yorkshire Moors by Elizabeth Ogilvie and Audrey Sleightholme.)

118   **THOMASON FOSS**   ☆☆☆

Goathland, North York Moors

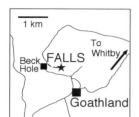

Maps: OS Landranger 94, OS Explorer OL Map 27.

Grid Ref: NZ 827022.

Nearest towns: Whitby 10 miles (16km), Pickering 14 miles (22km).

Walk: Grade – Moderate. Time – 15 mins each way.

Orientation: West.

The Falls: Eller Beck flows as a broad stream and narrows to about 3 metres between sandstone buttresses and falls 4 metres into a large, deep pool. The pool is partially surrounded by undercut sandstone cliffs. The boulders in the stream bed are slippery in the extreme. Above the falls is a bridge carrying the North Yorkshire Moors Railway across the beck.

Access: The hamlet of Beck Hole north of Goathland is a renowned beauty spot. Coming from Goathland, just before a steep hill down into Beck Hole, is a small car park identified by a waste bin. Park here and walk down into Beck Hole. Go past the inn, over the bridge and turn right along a footpath between the beck and the railway. This leads up to the falls.

Primrose

119   MALLYAN SPOUT   ☆☆☆

Goathland, North York Moors

Maps: OS Landranger 94, OS Explorer OL Map 27.

Grid Ref: NZ 824010.

Nearest towns: Whitby 9 miles (14km), Pickering 13 miles (21km).

Walk: Grade – Moderate. Time – 20 mins each way.

Orientation: West.

The Falls: Here you could be lost in a tropical jungle up a tributary of the Amazon or the Congo. The falls are reached by scrambling over slippery boul-

ders in the bed of West Beck. A small side stream falls as a veil of hundreds of thin strands in front of a vertical, moss-covered cliff. Everywhere the vegetation is lush. Ferns and moss drip with moisture and the valley is full of trees. Only dappled sunlight penetrates to the forest floor.

Access: Walk through the village of Goathland from bus stop, railway station or car park to the church. Follow a footpath opposite the church down to West Beck and turn left to the falls.

The North Yorkshire Moors Railway: The North Yorkshire Moors Railway runs from Pickering to Grosmont, along 18 miles of varied moorland and valley scenery, stopping at three stations on the way. Steam locomotives, lovingly maintained, provide the power to pull you up the steep gradients. If you've ever had a yen to drive a steam train then one of the short courses run by the railway would be for you. For those with other tastes Pullman trains provide luxury five course dinners en route during the summer.

120 NELLY AYRE FOSS

Goathland, North York Moors

Maps: OS Landranger 94, OS Explorer OL Map 27.

Grid Ref: SE 814997.

Nearest towns: Whitby 11 miles (18km), Pickering 14 miles (22km).

Walk: Grade – Moderate. Time – 10 mins each way.

Orientation: North.

The Falls: West Beck flows broadly over its sandstone bed. It drops over a wide shelf extending from bank to bank. In dry periods the beck divides into five separate streams. The banks show clearly alternating beds of sandstone and shale. A large fallen block of sandstone carries patterns surviving from when the last ripples disturbed the sand of a river delta in Jurassic times. Just upstream of the falls is a flat grassy area ideal for picnics.

Very little water flowing now

Access: From Goathland drive south-west past an inn (do not turn left here) and on to take a left fork along a 'no through road.' Park in a car park towards the end of this road two miles (3km) from Goathland. Walk back towards Goathland and take a footpath bearing left. This path goes on to reach the road again near New Wath Farm, but a sign to 'Foss' directs you down the hill to the beck and the waterfall. There is a bit of a scramble at the end.

121   RIGG MILL BECK FALLS   ☆☆☆

Whitby, North York Moors

Maps: OS Landranger 94, OS Explorer OL Map 27.

Grid Ref: NZ 908076.

Nearest towns: Whitby 2 miles (4km), Scarborough 18 miles (28km).

Walk: Grade – Moderate (muddy). 30 mins each way.

Orientation: North.

The Falls: At the confluence of two streams beside the footpath three falls can be seen. The main one drops vertically about three metres. They all lie within a valley filled with mixed deciduous woodland. The rock here is sandstone of the Ravenscar series laid down in a huge river delta in the Jurassic period. Old

tree trunks have weathered to fantastic shapes worthy of Henry Moore. A ten minute walk up the path along the right bank of the left hand stream reveals more falls deep in the valley. While in the area it is worth seeing the fine falls at Golden Grove, grid reference NZ 899089. These are on private land but can be seen from a footpath.

Access: Walk from Whitby or park in the village of Sneaton off the B1416 two miles south of Whitby. Walk east past the inn. Where the road becomes the access to a farm bear right along a muddy track between hedges. This drops down into the valley. Do not cross Rigg Mill Beck, but turn right and follow the path up the left bank to the falls.

122 FALLING FOSS and BLEA HILL BECK FALLS ☆☆☆

North York Moors

Maps: OS Landranger 94, OS Explorer OL Map 27.

Grid Ref: NZ 888035, NZ 895022.

Nearest towns: Whitby 5 miles (8km), Scarborough 16 miles (25km).

Walk: Grade – Each Moderate, Time – Each 5 mins each way.

Orientation: North-east and North-west.

The Falls: Falling Foss is seen from the footpath. It is possible to reach the top, but not the bottom of the falls. The beck runs over a lip of deeply fissured Dogger Sandstone rich in iron, down a sheer face of shale and into a deep plunge-pool. It then flows through a beautiful wooded valley with many mature beech trees. Blea Hill Beck Falls are seen best from a seat beside the higher footpath. The beck tumbles over complex sandstone ledges into a jumble of large stone blocks. The falls are surrounded by a variety of young trees, which may obscure them as they grow.

Falling Foss

Access: Take the B1416 road south from the village of Ruswarp south of Whitby or find the B1416 off the A171 Whitby to Scarborough road. At an angle on this road three other minor roads join (grid reference NZ 892046). For Falling Foss take the central one south-west to Falling Foss Car Park; for Blea Hill Beck Falls take the one leading south to Maybeck Car Park. The short walk down to Falling Foss is clearly signed. At Maybeck Car Park Blea Hill Beck joins May Beck from the right. High and low paths along the right bank of Blea Hill Beck lead to the falls. Other falls can be seen on May Beck.

The Hermitage and May Beck Nature Trail:

A ten-minute walk downstream from Falling Foss brings you to The Hermitage, a folly hewn out of solid rock. From Maybeck Car Park is the May Beck Trail, a nature trail with accompanying booklet published by North York Moors National Park.

The Hermitage

123   HAYBURN WYKE FALLS   ☆☆☆☆

Coast, North York Moors

Maps: OS Landranger 101, OS Explorer OL Map 27.

Grid Ref: TA 010971.

Nearest towns: Scarborough 7 miles (11km), Whitby 15 miles (24km).

Walk: Grade – Moderate, Time – 15 mins each way.

Orientation: East.

The Falls: These fine 5 metre high coastal falls usually consist of two streams split by a large sandstone block. When in spate, as in the illustration, that rock is covered by the volume of peaty water which sweeps down Hayburn Beck and the falls become one. The area is a nature reserve managed jointly by the National Trust and Yorkshire Wildlife Trust.

Access: Five miles north of Scarborough, along the a A171 towards Whitby, at Cloughton the road turns sharp left. At this point continue straight on along a minor road between the A171 and the coast. A turn-off to the right is signed to Hayburn Wyke Hotel. Patronise the hotel and use its car park. Follow the footpath into the oak woods that accompany the beck down to the sea. Sandstone steps which are relatively slip free even when wet lead down to the pebbly beach.

Yorkshire coast geology: The rock along this stretch of coast is part of the Ravenscar series of middle Jurassic sandstone deposited in the delta of a huge river flowing down from mountains to the north-west. Around the falls fossils of land plants such as liverworts, ferns and cycads that lived 180 million years ago may be found. This delta was covered by rising sea levels on at least three occasions and during those periods limestone containing marine fossils were laid down. On the beaches you may find fragments of jet.

Forest of Bowland, South Pennines & Peak District

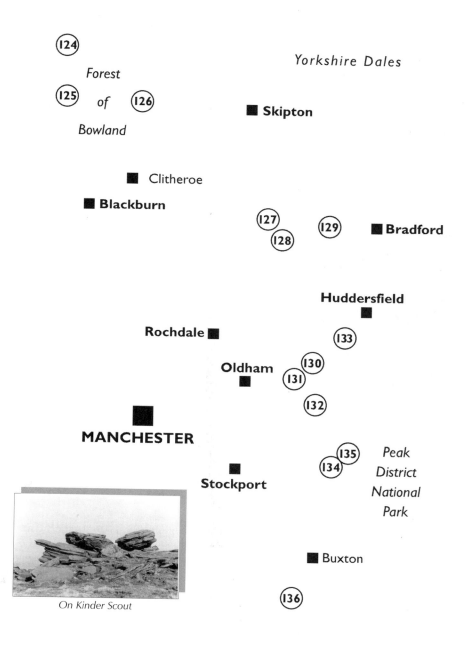

124

Forest

Yorkshire Dales

125 of 126

■ Skipton

Bowland

■ Clitheroe

■ Blackburn

127

128

129 ■ Bradford

Huddersfield ■

Rochdale ■

133

Oldham ■

130

131

132

MANCHESTER

■

Stockport

135

134

Peak District National Park

■ Buxton

136

On Kinder Scout

124   GOODBER BECK FALLS   ☆☆☆

Forest of Bowland

Maps: OS Landranger 97, OS Explorer OL Map 41.

Grid Ref: SD 612635.

Nearest towns: Kirkby Lonsdale 11 miles (17km), M6 Junction 34 11 miles (17km).

Walk: Grade – Moderate. Time – 10 mins each way.

Orientation: West.

The Falls: A real find. Having floundered about in Pedder Gill looking for waterfalls (very small) marked on the OS map I saw a figure I assumed was my wife and waved. The figure waved back. My wife won't like this, but the figure was an old shepherd who thought I was lost. He talked of many things, includ-

ing the waterfalls of the area, and pointed me to these. I am grateful to him. Goodber Beck falls 10 metres over a sandstone ledge, beneath which is shale, into a pool at the head of a short, but deep, ravine. The horse-shoe of cliffs around the falls is crowned with larch, oak and birch. The falls are just below a footbridge and are seen best from the left side.

Access: The B6480 road runs from the A683 at Hornby, through the villages of Wray, Wennington, Low Bentham and High Bentham to the A65(T) at Clapham. Turn into Wray, cross Wray Bridge and immediately turn right into a 'no through road'. This runs through woods along the banks of the River Roeburn then climbs onto open farmland. Follow it round Stauvin Farm and park beside the road just before it terminates at Harterbeck Farm. Walk on to Harterbeck Farm and turn left along a track. Cross a small beck by a flat stone bridge beside a ford. When the track swings left bear right keeping a wall to your right. A grassy track leads down to the wooden footbridge above the falls.

> ***Devastating floods:*** *Much damage was caused by floods in 1967 when 8 inches of rain fell in a few hours. Bridges and even cottages in Wray were swept away. Memorial gardens beside the river in Wray mark the spot where cottages once stood. Just like at Lynmouth in 1952, the devastation was caused by tree-trunks and debris being caught up by bridges that suddenly gave way, causing a surge of flood water to rush down the valley.*

125   TARNBROOK WYRE FALLS

Tarnbrook Fell, Forest of Bowland

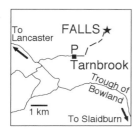

Maps: OS Landranger 102 and 103, OS Explorer OL Map 41.

Grid Ref: SD 612576.

Nearest towns: Lancaster 9 miles (14km), Clitheroe 18 miles (28km).

Walk: Grade – Moderate, Time – 1 hour each way.

Orientation: South-east.

The Falls: The Tarnbrook Wyre drains the high moorland of Tarnbrook Fell and joins with the Marshaw Wyre, which flows through the Trough of Bowland, to form the River Wyre. As it drops down from gritstone-capped

high fells it forms a series of attractive waterfalls. The furthest upstream is just below a small weir. The stream is forced through a gap in the rock only a foot wide and drops vertically between large sandstone blocks into a deep pool. About 150 metres downstream are two more falls and a slide down a huge ramp of rock. From the path there are distant views of Morecambe Bay.

Access: The Forest of Bowland is divided into northern and southern halves by a minor road from Abbeystead to Dunsop Bridge and Slaidburn. In summer this is a popular area for picnics along the banks of the Marshaw Wyre. From Abbeystead take a minor road to the hamlet of Tarnbrook and park there. A map board shows permitted paths on the fells. Follow a well-kept stone-chip track up Tarnbrook Fell. The track terminates at a turning circle but a path leads on to the falls.

See colour plate 7A

126   BOTTOMS BECK FALLS   ☆☆☆

Stocks Reservoir, Forest of Bowland

Maps: OS Landranger 103, OS Explorer OL Map 41.

Grid Ref: SD 745566

Nearest towns: Slaidburn 5 miles (8km), Settle 13 miles (21km).

Walk: Grade – Moderate, difficult final scramble. Time – 30 mins each way.

Orientation: South.

The Falls: Here is a series of four woodland falls in the Gisburn Forest. The middle two falls are in quick succession. Although not high, each is barely two metres, they form a delightful picture as they tumble over sandstone ledges

which dip back towards the falls. Each has a small plunge pool.

Access: Park in Stocks Reservoir car park near the north end of the reservoir on the edge of Gisburn Forest. Walk a few yards south-east along the road, enter the forest on the side away from the reservoir and follow the path parallel with the road until a forest track is reached with posts marked with red and blue bands. Walk along this easy track and after about 20 minutes look for two red and blue marker posts where two small paths lead off to the right within a few metres of each other. Take the second path. Where it enters a cutting with a hillside to the left and a bank to the right go over the bank and down to the falls.

> ***Attractions of Stocks Reservoir:*** *Stocks Reservoir car park is the site of the church of the inundated village of Stocks in Bowland. The church was dismantled and rebuilt as St James's Church one km to the south. Stocks Reservoir is one of the best wildfowl sites in the north-west of England. About 30 species are seen here each winter.*

127 LUMB SPOUT ☆☆☆

The Forest of Trawden, Lancashire, South Pennines

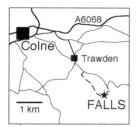

Maps: OS Landranger 103, OS Explorer OL Map 21.

Grid Ref: SD 921373.

Nearest towns: Colne 2 miles (3km), Burnley 9 miles (14km).

Walk: Grade – Moderate. Time – 30 mins round trip.

Orientation: West.

The Falls: Do not confuse these with Lumb Falls. 'Lumb' in Lancashire means 'pool'. This is an unexpectedly peaceful and secluded spot very close to industrial towns. Trawden Brook emerges from a cleft to fall eight metres almost vertically into a pool overhung with ash, oak, sycamore, alder and hazel. Above the fall the brook has carved a sinuous channel ('strid') through the rock.

Access: At a roundabout on the A6068 on the east side of Colne, follow the road signed to Trawden. This is the B6250. Drive through Trawden and park near the mill. Alternatively walk the minor road from Colne to Trawden. Walk along the road opposite the mill past some houses until a stile is seen in the wall on the left with a white sign indicating a footpath. Go through the stile, cross a field diagonally, go over a stream by a wooden footbridge and continue to the falls. To return climb to the top of the falls, cross a field to a farm and walk down the road to Trawden.

128   LUMB FALLS   ☆☆☆

West Yorkshire, South Pennines

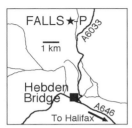

Maps: OS Landranger103, OS Explorer OL Map 21.

Grid Ref: SD 992314.

Nearest towns: Hebden Bridge 3 miles (5km), Halifax 10 miles (16km).

Walk: Grade – Easy. Time – 5 mins each way.

Orientation: South.

The Falls: Here is a lush oasis in bleak moorland country. Crimsworth Dean Beck flows through open moorland and falls over a ledge of millstone grit underlain with shale to enter the wooded valley of Crimsworth Dean leading down to Hebden Bridge. The plunge-pool is large enough for a swim. Above the falls is a fine larch tree, below are mainly birch and sycamore. An ancient pack-horse bridge spans the beck just above the falls.

Access: Take the A6033 road north from Hebden Bridge towards Haworth. After about 3 km, bear left along Old Road and, 1 km further, park beside the road at a bridleway sign on the left. Follow this steep bridlepath paved with millstone grit down to the falls.

> *Lime trails:* The packhorse bridge above the falls is on the lime trail. Limestone was heated in kilns near to where it was quarried to produce lime. This was then transported in panniers on horses from the Yorkshire Dales to farms in Calderdale to improve the fertility of the acid soil.

129   GOIT STOCK FALLS   ☆☆☆☆

Near Bradford, West Yorkshire

Maps: OS Landranger 104, OS Explorer OL Map 21.

Grid Ref: SE 077366.

Nearest towns: Bingley 2 miles (4 km). Bradford 6 miles (10km).

Walk: Grade – Moderate. Time – 25 mins each way.

Orientation: North.

The Falls: Here Harden Beck forms an impressive fall. The beck carries a good volume of water and the falls are about 4 metres wide and 5 metres tall. The majority of the fall is stepped, but on the left side the water falls unimpeded into a large plunge pool. The lip of the fall is sandstone and huge slabs of sandstone litter the bed of the stream below the falls. A few metres upstream are further pleasant, but smaller, falls. This valley with its waterfalls is an unexpected oasis of natural beauty close to heavily populated areas.

Access: Turn off the B6429 road at Harden between Bingley and Cullingworth north-west of Bradford. Park at and patronise The Malt Shovel. Cross the road and walk up Goit Stock Lane through a caravan park. Another 10 minutes walk along the path beside the beck and the falls are reached.

130   WESSENDEN BROOK FALLS

Wessenden Moor, Peak District

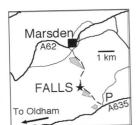

Maps: OS Landranger 110, OS Explorer OL Map 1.

Grid Ref: SE 055087.

Nearest towns: Huddersfield 7 miles (11km), Oldham 11 miles (16km).

Walk: Grade – Moderate. Time – 45 mins each way.

Orientation: North.

The Falls: The brook falls for about 12 metres down steep sandstone terraces into a small pool. Below this the stream flows around a jumble of large angular boulders. The striking feature of these falls is that they are flanked with banks of rhododendron.

Access: In Marsden on the A62 south-west of Huddersfield park at the lower end of Binn Road. Binn Road is found at a round-about with Mount Road, Fall Lane and Carr Road. On the right a sign reads "Public Foot-path to Wessenden Valley". Follow this path between tall mill buildings. When the base of a dam is reached climb a flight of about 200 steps to the top of the dam. Continue along the bank of Butterley Reservoir and Blakeley Reservoir. Do not drop into the valley along the Pennine Way, but keep to the main path until the falls are seen across the valley. The falls are reached by crossing the dam of Wessenden reservoir and taking a small path down to the falls or following farm track below Wessenden Lodge.

Rhododendron: *Although spectacular when in flower rhododendrons appear out of place on a Pennine moor. They are remarkably invasive, difficult to eradicate and poison the ground, making it more difficult for native species to get re-established. To my mind they should be confined and properly controlled in gardens.*

131   BIRCHEN CLOUGH FALLS

Saddleworth Moor, Peak District

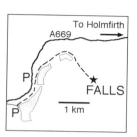

Maps: OS Landranger 110, OS Explorer OL Map 1.

Grid Ref: SE 038047.

Nearest towns: Oldham 6 miles (10km), Huddersfield 13 miles (21km).

Walk: Grade – Mostly easy with scramble at the end. Time – 1 hour each way.

Orientation: North-west.

The Falls: Many words around the country mean 'a small valley'. One such is 'clough' in this area. This changes to 'cleugh' in Scotland and Northumberland. In Birchen Clough are a number of waterfalls. The first is seen from the entrance to the clough at the North-west Water weir. The water

falls in two broken columns and continues over numerous ledges below the fall. A short scramble upstream reveals a small, but attractive fall where the stream curls round the base of a huge angular boulder. There are fine views of Raven Stones Brow, a high crag towering to the west.

Access: Park in Binn Green car park off the A635 just 5km east of Oldham where there are toilets including for disabled use, or in the nearby car park by the dam of Dovestone Reservoir. Follow the North West Water Authority road along the banks of Yeoman Hey and Greenfield Reservoirs keeping the water to your right. Follow the road beyond Greenfield Reservoir to a complex of weirs. Bear right up Birchen Clough.

132 CROWDEN LITTLE BROOK FALLS and HEY CLOUGH FALLS

Longdendale, Derbyshire, Peak District

Maps: OS Landranger 110, OS Explorer OL Map 1.

Grid Ref: SE 074023.

Nearest towns: Glossop 6 miles (10km), Sheffield 23 miles (37km).

Walk: Grade – Moderate. Time – 1 hour 5 mins each way.

Orientation: West and East.

The Falls: There are three falls close together on Crowden Little Brook. The waterfall furthest upstream falls four metres over a sandstone ledge into a

small pool. A stream in Meadow Clough joins Crowden Little Brook from the right in a fine 7 metre fall, again over sandstone with shale beneath. The sides of the fall are rich with heather. Just below the confluence of these two streams is a fall down a sandstone staircase with a cliff on the left.

Access: Park in a car park at Crowden off the A628(T) trans-Pennine road adjacent to a campsite and youth hostel. Bear right above the camp site into a road signed 'Langdendale Residential and Field Study Centre', then immediately bear right up a stone track which doubles back to the right. Go through a gate and along a path signed 'To Open Country'. Climb a stile (dog way provided) and bear left keeping a broken-down wall to your left. This is the only steep section of the walk. Go over another stile

(with dog way) noting quarry spoil heaps on the right. The path leads up the clough to the falls. The energetic may wish to walk to the falls in Hey Clough by taking an ill-defined path near the road by the youth hostel into a wood, then up into open country. The return trip to Hey Clough takes about 1 hour 10 mins. A pretty series of falls is the reward.

133   FOLLY DOLLY FALLS   ☆☆

West Yorkshire, South Pennines

Maps: OS Landranger 110, OS Explorer 288.

Grid Ref: SE 105114.

Nearest towns: Meltham <1 mile (1km), Huddersfield 6 miles (10km).

Walk: Grade – Moderate. Time – 10 mins each way.

Orientation: East.

The Falls: In dry weather these are intricate, lace like falls. Numerous thin streams cascade down gritstone ledges on a wide cliff into a shallow pool. The falls are hidden at the head of a gorge with overhanging oak and sycamore.

Access: From Meltham drive towards the village of Helme to the north-east. Just before the road turns left up the hill to enter the village there is a row of houses on the right. Park here. Between two houses opposite a track on the other side of the road is a gap leading to a small gate into a field. Go through this and continue in a straight line along the footpath down the hill. Cross a farm track then turn left along a disused railway until a stream passes under this embankment. Climb down to it and the falls are a few metres upstream.

Falls on a fault line: These falls are of considerable geological interest as they occur on a clearly visible fault line. The gritstone is a 10 metre thick bed called Huddersfield White Rock. This has been 'downthrown' bringing it into contact with a band of shale that has been eroded by the stream, leaving the hard gritstone cliff intact. This shale is seen on the right bank just below the falls.

134   KINDER DOWNFALL   ☆☆☆☆☆

Kinder Scout, Derbyshire, Peak District

Maps: OS Landranger 110, OS Explorer OL Map 1.

Grid Ref: SK 082889.

Nearest towns: Glossop 5 miles (8km), Sheffield 29 miles (47km).

Walk: Grade – Strenuous. Time – 4 hours round trip.

Orientation: South-west.

The falls in a south-westerly gale

The Falls: This waterfall is like no other in the country. It is best seen after heavy rain and preferably in a strong south-westerly gale. In dry weather the fall is reduced to a trickle. The stream drops into a huge chasm with vertiginous cliffs and littered with a chaotic jumble of great slabs and blocks of sandstone. In a high wind the whole waterfall can be blown up the cliff again.

Access: Take a good map and compass. The falls may be approached from Hayfield in the west or the south-east from Upper Booth. The westerly route is described. Park in the car park between Hayfield and Kinder Reservoir. Walk on, cross the river, take a footpath up its left bank, cross again and follow a footpath beside the gates across the road. When level with Kinder Reservoir turn left up the hillside then right along a path signed 'To the Snake Inn and to Edale'. The path leads up William Clough to join the Pennine Way. Turn right along the Pennine Way to Kinder Downfall. To return continue in the same direction. As soon as Red Brook is crossed take a small path half right (easy to miss) and follow it along the hillside until it drops down to a stile between two stone gateposts. Climb it and then climb another stile by the remains of a sheepfold and continue westward. After another stile head for a gate and stile at the far end of a field. Keep as straight as possible over two more stiles and join a farm road at Tunstead Clough Farm. The road leads to the car park.

Mass Trespass: *A plaque at the car park refers to The Mass Trespass onto Kinder Scout in April 1932. This was a turning-point in the struggle to open up vast areas of privately owned moorland for public recreation. It was a contentious issue then as now. Four hundred took part and five of their leaders were given prison sentences of two to six months. The peak National Park publishes a leaflet about this issue. Also see Freedom to Roam by Howard Hill, Moorland Publishing.*

135   **FAIR BROOK FALLS**   ☆☆

Snake Pass, Peak District

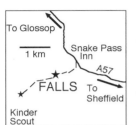

Maps: OS Landranger 110, OS Explorer OL Map 1.

Grid Ref: SK 107898.

Nearest towns: Glossop 7 miles (11km), Sheffield 17 miles (27km).

Walk: Grade – Moderate. Time – 30 mins each way.

Orientation: North-east.

The Falls: Fair Brook, which lives up to its name, forms a series of small waterfalls in an exceptionally pretty valley. The impressive crags of Fairbrook Naze and Seal Edge tower above the head of the clough. Side streams with their own waterfalls tumble down Middle Seal Clough and Upper Seal Clough adding to the charm of the scene. Birch trees provide shade and the moors are covered in heather and bilberries. It is a strenuous slog up the clough and onto the Kinder Scout Plateau. From here the view is magnificent, but the waterfall marked on maps at the head of the clough is insignificant except after heavy rain.

Access: Park at Snake Pass Inn on the A57 Sheffield to Glossop road and patronise the hostelry. Alternatively there is a lay-by about 300 metres down the hill. Climb a stile into a beech wood. The path leads down to a footbridge over the River Ashop. Fair Brook is a tributary of the River Ashop and the footpath runs up the left bank to the falls.

136 RIVER DANE FALLS ☆☆

Three Shire Heads, Peak District

Maps: OS Landranger 119, OS Explorer OL Map 24.

Grid Ref: SK 009685.

Nearest towns: Buxton 5 miles (8km), Leek 8 miles (13km).

Walk: Grade – Moderate. Time – 45 mins each way.

Orientation: South-east.

The Falls: The falls are at Three Shire Heads at the boundary of Staffordshire, Cheshire and Derbyshire. There are two falls, each just below stone-arched bridges, on two streams just before they join to form the River Dane. Two hundred metres downstream is a further attractive fall with a large plunge

Falls at Three Shire Heads

pool called Panniers Pool. Huge slabs of millstone grit form natural tables and chairs at this popular picnic site. On the hillside above is a stand of beech and pine.

Access: Park in Flash, the highest village in England at 1518 feet above sea-level, just off the A53 road between Buxton and Leek. Walk west along the higher road in the village to a stile on your right. Climb the stile and cross several fields and more stiles going steeply downhill to a footbridge across a stream. Continue up towards Wicken Walls farm and just before the farm turn right and then left along a tarmac road. The hillside to your right is littered with boulders of millstone grit. Pass a farm, keep right at a fork and then left at the next fork and take the path signed to Three Shire Heads. Follow this fairly rough track up to the falls.

Welsh Marches

■ Montgomery

⑬⑦ ■ Church Stretton

⑬⑧

Goodrich Castle

■ **Ludlow**

■ Knighton

■ Presteigne

Leominster ■

■ Hay-on-Wye

⑬⑨

⑭①

⑭⓪

■
Hereford

137   LIGHT SPOUT   ☆☆☆

Long Mynd, Shropshire, Welsh Marches

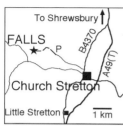

Maps: OS Landranger 137, OS Explorer 217.

Grid Ref: SO 430951.

Nearest Towns: Church Stretton 1 mile (2km), Shrewsbury 12 miles (19km).

Walk: Grade – Moderate. Time – 30 mins each way.

Orientation: South-east.

The Falls: These delightful falls are a popular tourist attraction. The falls, confined between rocky walls, drop into a small plunge-pool with high surrounds. A scramble up the side brings you to the top of the fall. The stream continues its turbulent course down Light Spout Hollow and on into Carding Mill Valley.

Access: Walk up Carding Mill Valley from Church Stretton (1 mile) or drive up the valley to the National Trust Centre or a car park a little further up. From the upper car park, cross the stream by a small wooden bridge and walk upstream to follow the path along the right bank. At the confluence of two streams cross the more southerly stream and walk up its left bank to the falls.

Local interest: These falls are on the Eastern slopes of the Long Mynd. There are footpaths leading up through the 'hollows', the name given to small valleys that cut deep into Long Mynd. These paths link up to form a network of tracks. Carding Mill Valley takes its name from a mill for carding wool, which was sited where the National Trust Centre now stands. In mediaeval times there was a water powered corn mill here.

138   OAKLEYMILL FALLS   ☆☆

Long Mynd, Welsh Marches

Maps: OS Landranger 137, OS Explorer 217.

Grid Ref: SO 429914.

Nearest towns: Church Stretton 2 miles (4km), Ludlow 14 miles (22km).

Walk: Grade – Moderate. Time – 10 mins each way.

Orientation: South.

The Falls: These falls are situated in a beautiful secluded valley off the beaten track. The falls are small, but attractive. On either side are outcrops of Precambrian sandstone with strata tilted almost vertically. These are some of the oldest rocks in England laid down 700 – 570 million years ago. The stream drops into a pool from which it escapes by a second fall. As the stream winds

down its valley there are flat grassy areas close to the water ideal for picnics. The valley is entered through bluebell woods on National Trust land.

Access: Two kilometres south of Church Stretton along the B4370 is the village of Little Stretton. From here take a minor road towards Minton and after just over one kilometre (just less than one mile) there is limited parking beside the road. Go over a stile beside a gate on the west side of the road where there is a sign that reads 'National Trust: Wern'. After a few yards bear right off the main track keeping close to a fence, climbing another stile then dropping down to the stream. The path runs beside the stream up to and beyond the waterfalls.

139   DULAS BROOK FALLS   ☆☆☆

Cusop Dingle, Herefordshire, Welsh Marches

Maps: OS Landranger 161, OS Explorer OL Map 13.

Grid Ref: SO 253397.

Nearest towns: Falls are at Hay-on-Wye, Hereford 22 miles (36km).

Walk: Grade – Moderate, scramble down to upper fall. Time – 1 hour each way.

Orientation: West and North-west.

The Falls: Cusop Dingle is a picturesque wooded valley with three falls along the course of Dulas Brook. The furthest of the three falls drops over a pale grey limestone cliff. The lush, steep-sided valley is home to enormous ferns. Oak

and coppiced hazel provide shade. Further downstream the brook divides over a wide, curved apron of rock and drops into a large pool with surrounding cliffs festooned with ferns and ivy. The lowest of the three falls is viewed from the road over a fence. The brook is squeezed between rocks and drops into a pool with an overhanging rock ledge on the left bank.

Access: Park in the car park by the Tourist Information Centre in Hay-on-Wye. Take the Bredwardine road, cross the brook and immediately turn right along the road up Cusop Dingle. Where the tarmac ends bear left through a gate labelled 'Brickyard Cottage' and follow the track across a field and into a wood. Where this track narrows to a single file footpath and swings left the upper falls are down to the right. An indistinct path leads down to them. This is a bit of a scramble.

> ***Books at Hay-on-Wye:*** *It is impossible to come to Hay-on-Wye without turning left from the car park to walk into the town and browse through the many second-hand bookshops. Some are general and others cater for specialist subjects. The knowledge stored in the heads of the booksellers is itself encyclopaedic. The Hay Festival of Literature and the Arts is held here in early summer.*

140   OLCHON BROOK FALLS   ☆☆☆

Olchon Valley, Herefordshire, Welsh Marches

Maps: OS Landranger 161, OS Explorer OL Map13.

Grid Ref: SO 268345.

Nearest towns: Hay-on-Wye 12 miles (19km), Abergavenny 15 miles (24km).

Walk: Grade – Moderate, Time – 15 mins each way.

Orientation: East.

The Falls: The Olchon Valley is a little known gem. The highest falls on Olchon Brook are just under the bridge at the start of the walk. However, they can only be viewed from above. The falls further upstream are in a steep-sided gully shaded by broad-leaved trees. The brook drops about 4 metres over jutting slabs of moss-covered sandstone rather like a row of irregular teeth.

Access: The village of Longtown is half way between Abergavenny and Hay-on-Wye and approached along a minor road. Drive north from Longtown and take a left fork to the Olchon Valley. A loop road runs up one side of the valley and back down the other. Park beside the road at the apex of this loop where the road crosses Olchon Brook. Follow a bridle track up the left bank of the brook to the end of the fence on your left. Open country has been reached. Drop down the hillside to the falls.

Woodland ecology: The woodland in the Olchon Valley used to be coppiced and supplied wood for the Lancashire clog industry and charcoal for the manufacture of gunpowder. Now the trees have grown up, shading the banks of the brook and discouraging the growth of grass. Consequently an excessive quantity of silt has entered the brook which in turn has been bad news for the trout which need clear water with a stony bed to the stream.

141   FALLS ON MONNOW AND CANDDO   ☆☆

Upper Monnow Valley, Welsh Marches

Maps: OS Landranger 161, OS Explorer OL Map 13.

Grid Ref: SO 265366, SO 282364.

Nearest towns: Hay-on-Wye 9 miles (15km), Abergavenny 16 miles (26km).

Walk: Grade – Moderate to Monnow, Easy to Canddo. Time – 5 mins and 3 mins each way.

Orientation: Both South-east.

The Falls: The falls on the infant River Monnow drop about 3 metres over horizontal slabs of red sandstone in a secluded valley and are viewed only from the right side. Other falls nearby are not accessible. The small fall on the

Falls on Canddo

Canddo, a tributary of the Monnow, falls as multiple streams and divides round an island dominated by a tall alder tree. There is pleasant flat grass beside the stream and an old lime kiln beside the path.

Access: Both falls are near Craswall on the minor road leading south from Hay-on-Wye to Longtown and eventually to Abergavenny. For the Monnow falls branch off up a side road at the Bull's Head at Craswall and park where the tarmac ends. Go through a gate into a field and down an ancient track to the falls. About 500 metres from the Bull's Head toward Hay-on-Wye park by St Mary's Church. A wide stone track snakes down the hill to the Canddo and the falls.

St Mary's Church: St Mary's Church stands in an empty field. Why are there no graves? The reason is the shallow soil and the hardness of the underlying rock. Against the north wall was either a fives court or a cockpit. A vertical stone there was either for recording scores or placing bets. Inside the church you can see a 15th century braced collar beam roof with unusual panelled soffit boards with vertical moulded ribs.

West Country

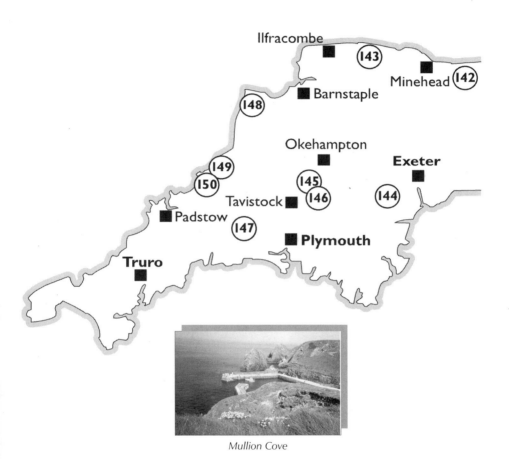

Ilfracombe

(143)

Minehead (142)

(148) Barnstaple

Okehampton

(149)

Exeter

(150)

(145)

Tavistock (146)

(144)

Padstow

(147)

Plymouth

Truro

Mullion Cove

142   FALLS IN BRENDON HILLS

Somerset, West Country

Maps: OS Landranger 181, OS Explorer OL Map 9.

Grid Ref: ST 017353, ST 026349.

Nearest towns: Minehead 16 miles (26km), Tiverton 19 miles (30km).

Walk: Grade – Moderate, difficult if overgrown. Time – 45 mins each way.

Orientation: Both North-east.

The Falls: These falls on tributaries of the Washford River which reaches the sea at Watchet are set deep in woodland. The fall in Western Cliff Wood has a near-vertical drop of 8 metres and is seen clearly from the path. The second

Eastern Wood Falls

fall in Eastern Wood is twice the height. The lower part is split into three streams by two large buttresses of rock. These falls will be seen and heard through the trees, but it may be difficult to get close to them because of dense undergrowth.

Access: The B3224 runs east – west about 5 miles from the coast near Minehead. At Sminhays Corner take a minor road to the north towards Roadwater for about 1 km and park at a disused slate quarry. Follow a zigzag forestry track down through the wood to the first falls. Continue along the track keeping close to two areas of open fields to your left to the second falls. There are several side-tracks to be avoided. It is best to follow the tracks on the OS Explorer OL Map 9 carefully.

143   WATERSMEET FALLS   ☆☆☆☆

North Devon, West Country

Maps: OS Landranger 180, OS Explorer OL Map 9.

Grid Ref: SS 744485.

Nearest towns: Linton and Lynmouth 2 miles (3km), Ilfracombe 20 miles (32km).

Walk: Grade – Moderate (steep steps). Wheelchair by arrangement (see below). Time – 5 mins each way.

Orientation: North.

The Falls: This is a popular beauty spot with good facilities. The principal falls are viewed from the footbridge across Hoar Oak Water near the café. These give a vivid impression of the power of this river. A short walk upstream brings you to a viewpoint for an impressive series of narrow falls and pools. Further along still, towards Hillsford Bridge, more falls are glimpsed through the trees. Downstream below the café there are attractive falls between rock buttresses where the river widens out. On the walk down to Lynmouth more small falls are seen.

Fall on Hoar Oak Water towards Hillsford Bridge

Access: Park in a car park at Watersmeet half a mile north of Hillsford Bridge towards Lynmouth on the A39. Steep steps lead down to the main falls and Watersmeet House owned by the National Trust. It is a shop, café and information centre. Wheelchair users can drive to the café by prior arrangement, tel: 01598 753348.

The floods of 1952:

The devastating floods and loss of life in Lynmouth on 15th August 1952 followed nine inches of rain in 24 hours on Exmoor. Bridges acted as dams for trees and boulders swept down by the river and when they gave way the sudden surges added to the devastation. Bridges have been rebuilt high above the water, or designed to be swept away themselves rather than act as obstructions.

144 **BECKY FALLS** ☆☆☆

Mid-Devon, West Country

Maps: OS Landranger 191, OS Explorer OL Map 28.

Grid Ref: SX 761801.

Nearest towns: Newton Abbot 9 miles (14km), Okehampton 20 miles (32km).

Walk: Grade – Easy with wheelchair access to main falls, easy/moderate to lower falls. Time – 10 mins to main falls, further 10 mins to lower falls.

Orientation: South-east.

The Falls: These are the falls for a family outing. Becka Brook (Becka or Becky) tumbles round and over piles of huge round granite boulders. There are separate upper and lower falls. Becky Falls Woodland Park is a Site of Special Scientific Interest. The mature trees include oak, beech, silver birch, holly and hazel.

Access: The falls are found four miles west of Bovey Tracey along a minor road towards Manaton. The paths are well-signed and maps are provided. Access to the top of the upper falls and along a path down the right bank is easy. You need stout shoes to visit the lower falls or follow the path along the left bank.

Facilities at Becky Falls: The woodland park with access to the falls is open for February half-term holiday and then mid-March until the end of October. To confirm please telephone 01647 221259. There is ample car parking, toilets, a restaurant, a shop selling gifts and crafts, tame goats, rabbits, sheep, ponies and rescued owls and other birds of prey. There is a variety of woodland trails.

145   WHITE LADY WATERFALL   ☆☆☆☆☆

Mid-Devon, West Country

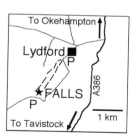

Maps: Os Landranger 191 and 201, OS Explorer OL Map 28.

Grid Ref: SX 501833.

Nearest towns: Tavistock 9 miles (14km), Okehampton 9 miles (15km).

Walk: Grade – Moderate. Time – 2 hours round trip. (15 mins each way from south entrance).

Orientation: North.

The Falls: Lydford Gorge (National Trust) contains several waterfalls. The White Lady Fall towards the southern end of the gorge is where the smaller River Burn falls 30 metres to join the larger River Lyd in the floor of the gorge. The River Lyd with greater erosive force then the Burn scooped out a deeper course for itself leaving the Burn in a hanging valley and creating this beautiful fall. The name White Lady is most appropriate. The graceful slender white falls contrast sharply with the surrounding dark slates. In the floor of the gorge the River Lyd flows fast and furiously zig-zagging through pot-holes to form Tunnel Falls and the Devil's Cauldron.

Access: Lydford Gorge is off the A386 between Tavistock and Okehampton. The National Trust levies a charge to visit the gorge which is reduced for those who arrive by public transport. There are car parks at the North (main) and South entrances. The North entrance is closed during winter months, but White Lady falls can still be visited via the South entrance. It is recommended that you enter from the north, take the high level path to the southern end, then follow the River Lyd back along the gorge. White Lady waterfall is much nearer the South entrance.

The Gubbinses: The gorge was home and refuge in the 16th century to the Gubbinses, a family of notorious outlaws under their leader Roger Rowle. They are supposed to have survived by sheep and cattle rustling and avoided capture by living in the inaccessible reaches of Lydford Gorge. They feature in Charles Kingsley's novel Westward Ho!

See colour plate 8

146 COLLY BROOK FALLS ☆☆

Dartmoor, West Country

Maps: OS Landranger 191 and 201, OS Explorer OL Map 28.

Grid Ref: SX 522775.

Nearest towns: Tavistock 4 miles (6km), Okehampton 16 miles (25km).

Walk: Grade – Moderate. Time – 5 mins each way.

Orientation: West.

The Falls: Colly Brook tumbles over a series of pretty falls in a valley shaded by silver birch and sycamore, flowing over and round large boulders covered in luxuriant moss. In places the stream divides around small islands. This is an ideal picnic spot providing sun and shade.

Access: Three miles north-east of Tavistock is the small village of Peter Tavy. Just north of the church turn right along a 'no through road' and park in a disused quarry beside the road. From here a track leads up the hill signed to Stephen's Grave and White Tor. Walk down the hill opposite this track to a gate and a footpath signed to The Combe. This leads straight down to the falls. The path can be followed on to Peter Tavy.

Marchant's Cross

Dartmoor crosses: *Seven miles south-east of Tavistock near the village of Meavy stands Marchant's Cross. This is one of over 130 crosses on Dartmoor. Some are relatively modern, having been erected within the last 100 years, others may be over 1000 years old. They served a variety of functions. Some marked the boundaries of estates, others were erected as way-markers across the bleak moorland. They were certainly used as such by monks travelling between the Abbeys of Tavistock, Buckland and Buckfast. Crosses served the same purposes on other remote moorland areas such as the North Yorkshire Moors. Some of the more modern crosses were raised as memorials or to mark special occasions. Although there are several theories the original purpose of Marchant's Cross is lost in antiquity.*

147 GOLITHA FALLS ☆☆☆

Fowey Valley, Bodmin Moor, West Country

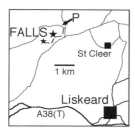

Maps: OS Landranger 201, OS Explorer 109.

Grid Ref: SX 222686.

Nearest towns: Liskeard 4 miles (6km), Bodmin 12 miles (19km).

Walk: Grade – Moderate. Time – 15 mins each way.

Orientation: South-west.

The Falls: The Rover Fowey flows along the floor of a wooded valley forming a series of small waterfalls and rapids over granite boulders. The path runs along the river bank giving easy access and good views of the falls. The granite intrusion through sedimentary rocks is seen at the lower end of the falls. Salmon, otters and numerous species of birds and butterflies are found in this nature reserve. Less spectacular, but just as important, are the species of moss and lichen that thrive in the damp environment around the falls. Golitha National Nature Reserve is administered by English Nature together with Caradon Moorland Countryside Service.

Access: The car park at the head of the reserve is four miles north-west of Liskeard approached along minor roads. Alternatively reach it from the north leaving the A30(T) at Bolventor (Jamaica Inn) on Bodmin Moor and drive along the attractive valley of the River Fowey. The path is well-signed.

> *Golitha falls were different once: The word Golitha means obstacle. A huge boulder used to obstruct the river forming an impressive waterfall. This was blown up in the 19th century to allow salmon to swim further upstream to spawn. Look out for signs of previous copper mining in the valley. The mine was only productive for a few years in the mid-19th century.*

> *See colour plate 7B*

148 SPEKE'S MILL MOUTH WATERFALL ☆☆☆☆☆

North Devon Coast, West Country

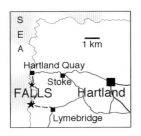

Maps: OS Landranger 190, OS Explorer 126.

Grid Ref: SS 224235.

Nearest towns: Bideford 16 miles (25km), Bude 17 miles (27km).

Walk: Grade – Moderate. Time – 20 mins each way.

Orientation: North and North-west.

The Falls: This is the most dramatic coastal waterfall in England. A stream that meanders through a pleasant green valley suddenly plunges over an almost vertical cliff of dark grey stone. It then turns and drops as twin falls again to the stony beach. The main falls can be seen without scrambling down to the

bottom. Between Speke's Mill Mouth and Hartland Quay are smaller but attractive coastal falls at Saint Catherine's Tor.

Access: Park at the car park at Hartland Quay. Take the coastal path in a southerly direction and within a few minutes the falls at Saint Catherine's Tor are reached. Climb down to the beach with the aid of a rope placed for that purpose. After climbing up again walk along the coastal path to Speke's Mill Mouth one mile south of Hartland Quay. An alternative approach is to park at Lymebridge (Grid Ref: SS 236228). At the crossroads follow the road west and very soon take a stony path on the right. (You may be able to park here.) Follow this path down to the falls and the sea. While here visit Docton Mill Gardens.

How these coastal falls were formed: The falls along this stretch of coastline are the best examples in England of sea erosion truncating the valleys and producing waterfalls at the coast. The sea is removing the land faster than the waterfalls can cut their way upstream. In some places the sea has eroded into the side of a valley, trapping the river, and leaving a dry valley beyond. The rocks here are metamorphic rocks of the Carboniferous Period. The dramatic folding of these rocks under intense pressure is seen clearly in the cliffs at Hartland Quay.

149   PENTARGON FALLS   ☆☆☆

˙Cornish Coast, West Country

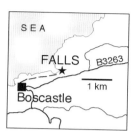

Maps: OS Landranger 190, OS Explorer 111.

Grid Ref: SX 108919.

Nearest towns: Falls are at Boscastle, Camelford 6 miles (10km).

Walk: Grade – Moderate. Time – 30 mins each way.

Orientation: West.

The Falls: The stream flows through a steep sided valley then drops over a high vertical cliff to a beach of rocks and grey sand. This fine waterfall is seen from the South-west Coast Path. There is no access down to the beach. With a strong westerly wind the water is blown back up the cliff.

Burnet Rose that grows along the coast path

Access: From Boscastle follow the South-west Coast Path eastward for about 2 km until the falls are reached. There are 182 steps down to the top of the falls. It is possible to park in a lay-by on the B3263 one kilometre east of Boscastle from where a footpath leads down to the South-west Coast Path where you turn right to the falls. This halves the walking time but does not avoid the 182 steps!

150

ST NECTAN'S WATERFALL and ROCKY VALLEY FALLS

☆☆☆☆

Cornwall, West Country

Maps: OS Landranger 190 and 200, OS Explorer 111.

Grid Ref: SX 081885.

Nearest towns: Wadebridge 16 miles (25km), Bude 16 miles (25km).

Walk: Grade – Moderate. Time – 30 mins each way.

Orientation: West.

The Falls: A natural rock bridge makes these falls unusual and attractive. The stream has cut a channel in the rock less than one metre wide, then drops about 13 metres into a plunge pool from which it escapes, through an almost circular hole beneath a diagonal rock arch, to drop again down to the valley floor. Around the falls are vertical or overhanging cliffs festooned with moss, ferns and trailing ivy. The deep plunge-pool is known as St Nectan's Kieve, being the Cornish word for a basin. Along the well-named Rocky Valley towards the sea are two falls in quick succession. The rough rock has been polished smooth in the stream bed.

Access: Park at the Rocky Valley Centre at Trethevy on the B3263 1½ miles east of Tintagel. Here there are toilets, a café and shop. Take the road to the left of the centre which becomes a footpath through the picturesque St Nectan's Glen and leads to the falls where there is a small café and a fee to be paid to view the falls. For the Rocky Valley Falls take a footpath down to the sea from the B3263 past the Miller Restaurant. The Coastal Path crosses this path just above the falls.

Ancient history: This area is rich in ancient history and legend. St Nectan, a Celtic saint and son of St Brechan, built a hermitage near the top of the waterfall in about AD 500. In Rocky Valley, by the ruined Trewethet Mill, are two labyrinth carvings on a rock, probably dating from the early bronze age 1800 – 1400 BC.

Additional waterfalls

These are not mentioned in the main text, but are worth seeing. *denotes access for wheelchairs

Name	Star rating	Area	OS Landranger	Grid reference
Angletarn Beck Falls	☆☆	Lake District	90	NY 407140
Arten Gill Falls	☆☆	Yorkshire Dales	98	SD 778858
Ashfold Side Beck Falls	☆	Yorkshire Dales	99	SE 108661
Baysdale Beck Tributary Falls*	☆	North York Moors	94	NZ 652074
Ben Gill Falls	☆☆	LakeDistrict	89	NY 088148
Black Force	☆	North Pennines	91 and 92	NY 961313
Blackden Brook Falls	☆☆	Peak District	110	SK 122884
Brandy Gill Falls	☆☆	Lake District	90	NY 323334
Brimful Beck Falls	☆☆☆	Lake District	89	NY 164084
Brontë Falls	☆	South Pennines	103	SD 998357
Browney Gill Falls	☆☆	Lake District	89 and 90	NY 265043
Buckbarrow Beck Falls	☆☆	Lake District	96	SD 137911
Buttertubs Falls	☆	Yorkshire Dales	98	SD 874961
Caiston Beck Falls	☆☆	Lake District	90	NY 393097
Caudale Beck Falls	☆☆	Lake District	90	NY 406115
Combe Gill Beck	☆☆☆	Lake District	89 and 90	NY 252131
Cosh Beck Falls	☆	Yorkshire Dales	98	SD 870774
Cragside Estate Falls	☆	Northumbria	81	NU 090016
Crooked Clough Falls	☆☆	Peak District	110	SK 093942
Crowden Brook Falls	☆☆	Peak District	110	SK 102862
Daddry Shield Burn Falls	☆☆	Northumbria	91 and 92	NY 893375
Dean Beck Falls*	☆	South Pennines	104	SE 003404
Deepdale Beck Falls	☆	North Pennines	92	NZ 032163
Devil's Water Falls*	☆☆	Northumbria	87	NY 975635
Disher Force	☆	Yorkshire Dales	98	SD 979905
Docker Force	☆☆☆	Lake District	91	NY 585088
East Dart River Falls	☆☆	West Country	191	SX 627811
East Okement River Falls	☆	West Country	191	SX 607940
Flinter Gill Falls	☆☆	Yorkshire Dales	98	SD 702865
Flushiemere Beck Falls	☆☆	Northumbria	91 and 92	NY 908293
Force Jump	☆☆	Lake District	90	NY 461044
Foss Gill Falls	☆☆	Yorkshire Dales	103	SD 912596
Gate Gill Beck Falls	☆	Lake District	90	NY 324262
Gorpley Clough Falls	☆☆	South Pennines	103	SD 917235
Grassguards Gill Spout	☆☆	Lake District	96	SD 225977
Great Grain Gill Falls	☆	Lake District	90	NY 492095
Green Burn Falls	☆☆☆	Lake District	90	NY 324101
Greenhead Gill Falls	☆☆	Lake District	90	NY 348085
Greenless Hole Falls	☆☆	North Pennines	92	NZ 057278
Green's Clough	☆	South Pennines	103	SD 892260
Greenup Syke Falls	☆	Lake District	89 and 90	NY 245175
Grindsbrook Falls	☆☆	Peak District	110	SK 117872
Grisedale Beck Falls	☆☆☆	Lake District	90	NY 360141
Gudham Gill Falls	☆	North Pennines	86	NY 782450

Name	Rating	Region	Page	Grid Ref
Hard Level Force	☆☆	Yorkshire Dales	91 and 92	NY 968008
Hebblethwaite Gill Falls	☆☆	Yorkshire Dales	98	SD 703931
Hen Hole Falls✚	☆☆?	Northumbria	74	NT 887203
Hopgill Beck Falls	☆☆☆	Lake District	90	NY 482116
Horton Gill Beck Falls	☆	Yorkshire Dales	98	SD 905885
How Beck Falls	☆	North Pennines	91 and 92	NY 972186
Hudeshope Beck Falls*	☆☆	Northumbria	91 and 92	NY 947268
Ibbeth Peril	☆☆	Yorkshire Dales	98	SD 742865
Keld Scar Waterfalls	☆	Yorkshire Dales	98	SD 916861
Kilnhow Beck Falls	☆	Lake District	90	NY 316258
Liza Beck Falls	☆☆	Lake District	89 and 90	NY 184215
Low Beck Falls	☆☆☆	Lake District	89	NY 152135
March Haigh Reservoir Falls	☆☆	South Pennines	110	SE 018128
Mir Gill Beck Falls*	☆	North Pennines	91 and 92	NY 901181
Mosedale Beck Falls	☆☆	Lake District	90	NY 347224
Nelly Force	☆	Yorkshire Dales	98	SE 039915
Pull Beck Falls	☆☆	Lake District	90	NY 345017
Ravensbeck Falls	☆☆	North Pennines	86	NY 612435
Rayrigg Cascades*	☆☆	Lake District	96 and 97	NY 404976
Redmire Force	☆☆	Yorkshire Dales	98	SE 044901
Ridge End Burn Falls	☆	Northumbria	80	NY 659956
River Hodder Tributary Falls	☆	Forest of Bowland	103	SD 722527
River Wenning Falls	☆	Forest of Bowland	97	SD 657691
River Wharfe Falls*, Langstrothdale	☆☆	Yorkshire Dales	98	SD 892797
Rowantreethwaite Beck Falls	☆☆	Lake District	90	NY 482118
Rush Gill Beck Falls	☆☆	Lake District	90	NY 368209
Scale Beck Falls	☆☆☆	Lake District	89 and 90	NY 213024
Scale Close Force	☆☆☆	Lake District	89 and 90	NY 245147
Scandale Beck Falls	☆☆	Lake District	90	NY 379067
Scow Force*	☆	Yorkshire Dales	98	SD 773853
Sills Burn Falls	☆	Northumbria	80	NY 815038
Shoulthwaite Gill Falls	☆☆☆	Lake District	89 and 90	NY 298188
Spen Gill Falls	☆☆	Howgill Fells	98	SD 699998
Stanhope Burn Tributary Falls	☆☆	Northumbria	87	NY 986410
Stannah Gill Falls	☆☆	Lake District	90	NY 327189
Strands Beck Falls	☆	North Pennines	91	NY 736258
Thornthwaite Force	☆☆	Lake District	90	NY 511159
Tidna Falls	☆☆	West Country	190	SS 195148
Torver Beck Falls	☆☆	Lake District	96 and 97	SD277960
Trout Beck Falls	☆☆	Lake District	90	NY 418066
Trout Beck Falls*	☆☆	North Pennines	91	NY 758336
Upper River Rye Falls	☆☆	North York Moors	100	SE 513963
Welcombe Mouth Falls*	☆☆	West Country	190	SS 212180
West Dipton Burn Falls	☆☆	Northumbria	87	NY 913614
Whillan Beck Falls	☆☆	Lake District	89 and 90	NY 185025
White Moss Common Falls*	☆☆	Lake District	90	NY 351066
Wintergroove Gill Falls	☆☆	Lake District	90	NY 361192
Woody Bay Falls	☆☆☆	West Country	180	SS 677489
Wray Gill Falls	☆☆	Lake District	90	NY 325073

✚ The only waterfall in this book I have not yet visited

Bibliography

The following books are useful sources of information.

General

Waterfall Walks Teesdale and The High Pennines, Mary Welsh, Pub. Cicerone Press, ISBN 1-85284-158-3

Walks to Yorkshire Waterfalls, Mary Welsh, Pub. Cicerone Press, ISBN 1-85284-062-5

More Walks to Yorkshire Waterfalls, Mary Welsh, Pub. Cicerone Press, ISBN 1-85284-091-9

Waterfalls of Craven, Pip Seymour, Pub. Lee Press, ISBN 0-9524727-0-8

A Naturalist's Guide to Lakeland Waterfalls throughout the year, Mary Welsh, Pub. Westmorland Gazette, ISBN 0-9022-72-616

A Second Naturalist's Guide to Lakeland Waterfalls throughout the year, Mary Welsh, Pub. Westmorland Gazette, ISBN 0-902272-65-9

A Third Naturalist's Guide to Lakeland Waterfalls throughout the year, Mary Welsh, Pub. Westmorland Gazette, ISBN 0-902272-73-X

A Fourth Naturalist's Guide to Lakeland Waterfalls throughout the year, Mary Welsh, Pub. Westmorland Gazette, ISBN 0-902272-80-2

Geology

Teach Yourself Geology, David A. Rothery, Pub. Hodder Headline Plc, ISBN 0-340-67992-1

Geology and Scenery in Britain, John Whittow, Pub. Chapman Hall, ISBN 0-412-44380-5

Geography. An Integrated Approach, David Waugh, Pub. Thomas Nelson and Sons Ltd, ISBN 0-17-444065-0

The Physical Geography of Landscape, Roy Collard, Pub. Unwin Hyman Ltd, ISBN 0-7135-2734-X

Origins. The evolution of continents, oceans and life, Ron Redfern, Pub. Cassell and Co, ISBN 0-304-35403-1

Lakeland Rocky Rambles, Bryan Lynas, Pub. Sigma Leisure, ISBN 1-85058-396-X

Flora and Fauna

The Biology of Streams and Rivers, Paul S. Giller and Björn Malmquist, Pub. Oxford University Press, ISBN 0-19-854978-4

Along the Riverbank, The Living Countryside, Consultant – Nigel Holmes, Pub. Readers Digest, ISBN 0-276-39294-9

The Ecology of Running Waters, H. B. N. Hynes, Pub. Liverpool University Press,

Collins guide to the Ferns, Mosses and Lichens of Britain and North and Central Europe, Hans Martin Jahns, Pub. Harper Collins, ISBN 00-02192543

Freshwater Fish of the British Isles, Nick Giles, Pub. Swan Hill Press, ISBN 1-85310-317-9

Uses of waterfalls

The Watermills of Britain, Leslie Syson, Pub. David and Charles Ltd, ISBN 0-7153-7824-4

The BP book of Industrial Archaeology, Neil Cossons, Pub. David and Charles Ltd, ISBN 0-7153-0134-9

Industrial Archaeology of The Lake Counties, J.D. Marshall and Michael Davies-Shiel, Pub. David and Charles Ltd, ISBN 7153-4695-4

Mines and Mining, John Postlethwaite, First published 1877 republished 1975 by Michael Moon at Beckernet Bookshop, Beckernet, Cumbria, ISBN 0-904131-10-6

The Transformation of Britain 1830 – 1939 G. E. Mingay, Pub. Routledge and Kegan Paul, ISBN 0-7100-9762-X

Waterfalls in Art

The Art and Architecture of China, Laurence Sickman and Alexander Soper, The Pelican History of Art, 3rd edition, Pub. Penguin Books, ISBN 0-300-05334-7

Observations, relative chiefly to Picturesque Beauty, made in the year 1772 on Several Parts of England; particularly the Mountains, and Lakes of Cumberland and Westmorland, William Gilpin MA, Facsimile reprint pub. Woodstock Books,

Dictionary of Art Ed. Jane Turner, Vol 18 Landscape Painting, Pub. Macmillan Publishers Ltd, ISBN 1-884446-00-0

Waterfalls in Poetry

The River's Voice, Edited by Angela King and Susan Clifford, Pub. Green Books Ltd, ISBN 1-870098-82-X

Index of waterfalls

Numbers refer to the waterfall numbers, not page numbers.
*denotes wheelchair access

Is this the future?

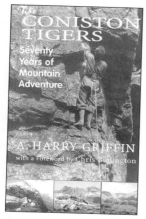

THE CONISTON TIGERS: Seventy Years of Mountain Adventure
A. Harry Griffin
Lakeland Book of The Year, 2000! The life story of
A. Harry Griffin MBE, Country Diary writer for *The Guardian*. "A very special book . . . a living history of Modern Lakeland climbing" – Chris Bonington. ***£9.95***

IN SEARCH OF SWALLOWS & AMAZONS
Roger Wardale
This is a revised edition of a popular book originally published in 1986. Additional material has been added to satisfy even the most avid reader of "Swallows & Amazons" – three decades of Ransome hunting with text and photographs to identify the locations of the ever-popular series of books. ***£7.95***

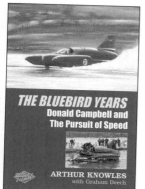

THE BLUEBIRD YEARS: Donald Campbell and the Pursuit of Speed
Arthur Knowles with Graham Beech
Fully revised account of Donald Campbell's attempts to raise the world water-speed record in "Bluebird" to 300mph. Includes recovery of the wreck and the funeral of Donald Campbell in 2001. "It's a damn good read and there are plenty of rare photos." – *Focus magazine* ***£9.95***

LEAP INTO LEGEND:Donald Campbell and the Complete Story of the World Speed Records
Steve Holter
This is the life story of the most famous British record breakers on land and water: Donald Campbell and his father, Sir Malcolm. It is also a story of the triumphs of British engineering between the two world wars - when huge and powerful aeroengines were being developed for the war effort, and ultimately used in peacetime to propel record-breaking cars and boats. ***£10.95***

ONLY A BLOODY GAME
Tony Rossiter
Based on real characters and incidents from the author's long but undistinguished career as a village cricketer, 'Only a Bloody Game' takes a tongue-in-cheek look at the grassroots of village cricket. Packed with yarns, jokes and excellent cartoons. ***£6.95***

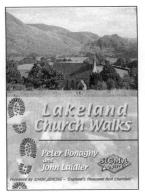

LAKELAND CHURCH WALKS

Peter Donaghy and John Laidler

Nominated for Lakeland Book of The Year, 2002 – and with a foreword by Simon Jenkins of *The Times*. 30 detailed circular walks ranging from 3½ to 12 miles with alternative shorter options, each starting from a noteworthy church. ***£8.95***

NORTHUMBRIA CHURCH WALKS

Peter Donaghy and John Laidler

International rock star, conservationist and Northumbrian **Sting** writes in the foreword to this book how he has so often found solutions to life's problems while on long, solitary walks in this unspoilt part of England, A selection of 30 walks with historical and cultural details of churches included with each walk. ***£8.95***

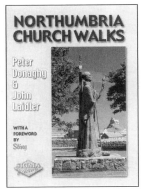

WALKS IN ANCIENT LAKELAND

Robert Harris

A collection of circular walks ranging in length from 2 to 10 miles, each visiting sites and monuments from the Neolithic and Bronze ages, linked where possible with ancient trackways. All walks are accompanied by sketch maps, and the author's intricate hand-drawn sketches. ***£6.95***

THE ABBEY TRAIL: over 100 miles of walks through Yorkshire's finest countryside

Clive Newsome

The Abbey Trail is an eight-day long-distance walk (with alternative circular day walks) through the beautiful Yorkshire countryside visiting some of England's greatest abbeys. Brief histories are provided for all places along the trail and detailed maps clearly outline all routes adding to the enjoyment. The Yorkshire countryside with its gently sloping hills and valleys make it ideal for walkers of all ages and abilities. ***£7.95***

All of our books are available from your local bookshop or from Amazon.co.uk. In case of difficulty, or to obtain our complete catalogue, please contact:
SIGMA LEISURE, 5 ALTON ROAD, WILMSLOW, CHESHIRE SK9 5DY
Phone/Fax: 01625-531035 E-mail: info@sigmapress.co.uk
For the latest news and a browsable updated, catalogue, visit us on the World Wide Web – **www.sigmapress.co.uk**